AF714464

SIDE EFFECTS OF ARTIFICIAL INTELLIGENCE

What AI Is Doing to Human Thought

Table of Contents

Introduction

Artificial Intelligence is no longer a distant concept discussed only in laboratories, science fiction novels, or speculative futurism. It is here—embedded quietly yet decisively in everyday life. From the moment a person wakes and checks a phone to the instant an algorithm recommends what to read, watch, buy, or believe, AI is already at work. It assists, predicts, filters, and decides. What makes this transformation unprecedented is not merely the speed at which AI has advanced, but the subtlety with which it has integrated itself into human thought processes.

This book does not approach Artificial Intelligence as a story of machines replacing jobs or robots overtaking society—topics that have already been widely debated. Instead, it examines a quieter and more profound consequence: the effect of AI on how humans think, reason, decide, remember, create, and understand themselves. The most significant side effects of AI are not always visible in factories or offices; they unfold internally, within the human mind.

Human intelligence evolved through struggle—through memory, trial and error, deep focus, imagination, and moral judgment. Today, many of these cognitive functions are being outsourced to machines. Navigation replaces spatial awareness. Recommendation engines replace curiosity. Automated answers replace reflection. Over time, convenience reshapes cognition. What begins as assistance can gradually become dependency, and dependency, when unnoticed, has consequences.

Artificial Intelligence is not neutral. It is trained, shaped, and optimized by human choices, economic incentives, and hidden objectives. Algorithms decide what information rises and what disappears, what voices are amplified and what ideas are buried. In doing so, they influence beliefs, emotions, and behavior. The human mind, exposed continuously to algorithmic curation, adapts—often without awareness. Thought patterns narrow. Attention fragments. Emotional responses become more predictable.

This book explores how AI alters creativity by favoring patterns over originality, how it reshapes decision-making by replacing intuition with statistical confidence, and how it influences emotional life by simulating understanding without possessing consciousness. It examines the psychological tension that arises when humans begin comparing their worth to machines designed to outperform them in speed, efficiency, and output. It also addresses the ethical dilemma of delegating judgment to systems that cannot bear responsibility.

Yet this is not an anti-technology manifesto. Artificial Intelligence, when understood and governed wisely, can enhance human potential rather than diminish it. The danger lies not in AI itself, but in unexamined dependence and unconscious surrender of agency. The purpose of this book is to illuminate the trade-offs we are making—often unknowingly—between efficiency and depth, speed and wisdom, automation and autonomy.

"Side Effects of Artificial Intelligence" invites readers to step back and observe how thinking itself is changing. It challenges the assumption that progress is always beneficial simply because it is advanced. As AI continues to evolve, the central question is no longer what machines can do—but what humans may slowly stop doing if they are not attentive. The future of intelligence is not only artificial; it is deeply human, and its direction remains a choice.

Chapter 1:
The Rise of Thinking Machines

For most of human history, tools were extensions of the hand. They amplified physical strength, increased efficiency, and reduced labor, but they never challenged the human role as the primary thinker and decision-maker. A hammer did not choose where to strike, and a calculator did not decide what question mattered. Artificial Intelligence represents a fundamental departure from this historical pattern. For the first time, tools are no longer limited to execution; they now participate in judgment.

The rise of thinking machines did not arrive with a dramatic announcement. There were no alarms signaling the moment when software began to influence reasoning. Instead, AI entered daily life quietly, disguised as convenience. Search engines offered faster answers. Recommendation systems simplified choices. Navigation apps reduced uncertainty. Each innovation appeared helpful, even liberating. Yet collectively, they marked a subtle shift: humans began deferring not just tasks, but thinking itself.

As AI systems improved, their role evolved from assistance to guidance. Algorithms now prioritize information, predict behavior, assess risk, and recommend actions across finance, healthcare, education, law enforcement, and personal life. Decisions once shaped by experience, intuition, and ethical reflection are increasingly influenced—or outright made—by data-driven systems. The authority of these systems is rarely questioned, largely because their processes remain invisible and their outputs appear objective.

This chapter examines how tools became decision-makers and why that transition matters. It explores the psychological comfort humans find in automated certainty and the cognitive trade-off that follows. When machines suggest, humans tend to comply. When systems optimize, individuals adapt. Over time, reliance transforms into trust, and trust becomes authority.

Understanding this shift is essential, because it defines the foundation upon which all later consequences of AI rest. Before examining how Artificial Intelligence reshapes creativity, attention, or identity, one must first understand how thinking machines earned their place—not by force, but by permission.

From Tools to Decision-Makers

For thousands of years, human progress has been defined by tools. From the stone axe to the printing press, from the steam engine to the computer, tools extended human capability without challenging human authority. They amplified strength, speed, memory, and reach, but they remained fundamentally passive. A tool waited for instruction. It responded to intention. Responsibility always rested with the human mind behind it.

Artificial Intelligence breaks this historical pattern.

Unlike traditional tools, AI systems do not merely execute commands; they evaluate options, detect patterns, predict outcomes, and recommend actions. In many cases, they make decisions independently once parameters are set. This shift—from execution to judgment—marks one of the most profound transformations in human-technology relationships. The tool no longer waits. It observes, learns, and acts.

Early digital tools were deterministic. A calculator followed explicit rules. A spreadsheet processed predefined formulas. Even early software systems required direct human input for every meaningful operation. AI, however, operates probabilistically. It does not follow fixed instructions in the traditional sense; it infers, adapts, and optimizes based on data. This gives it an appearance of intelligence that feels closer to human reasoning than mechanical computation.

As AI models grew more sophisticated, they moved into domains once considered exclusively human. Credit approval systems began evaluating trustworthiness. Medical algorithms started assisting in diagnoses. Hiring software filtered candidates before a human ever saw a résumé. Recommendation engines shaped what people read, watched, and believed. In each case, decision-making authority subtly shifted from people to systems.

What makes this transition especially powerful is its invisibility. AI rarely announces itself as a decision-maker. Instead, it presents outcomes as suggestions, rankings, scores, or probabilities. Humans remain "in the loop" nominally, but the cognitive framing changes. When a system highlights one option over others, it quietly defines what is reasonable, safe, or desirable. The human response is often to accept rather than to question.

This acceptance is reinforced by perceived objectivity. Machines, unlike humans, are assumed to be free from emotion, bias, and inconsistency. Data feels neutral. Numbers feel trustworthy. As a result, AI-driven decisions are often treated as superior to human judgment, even when they are trained on incomplete, biased, or historically flawed data. The authority of AI is not earned through wisdom, but through confidence.

Over time, repeated reliance reshapes behavior. When people consistently defer to algorithmic recommendations, they practice less independent evaluation. Judgment becomes reactive rather than reflective. Instead of asking "What do I think is right?", the question subtly shifts to "What does the system suggest?" This is not an immediate loss of autonomy, but a gradual erosion of cognitive initiative.

The transition from tools to decision-makers also changes accountability. Traditional tools could not be blamed for outcomes; responsibility was clear and direct. With AI systems, responsibility becomes diffuse. When an algorithm denies a loan, misidentifies a suspect, or prioritizes harmful content, accountability is often unclear. Is the fault with the developer, the data, the organization, or the system itself? This ambiguity weakens ethical responsibility while increasing systemic power.

Another critical dimension of this shift is scale. Human decision-making is limited by time, attention, and energy. AI systems operate continuously, across millions of users, in real time. A single algorithmic change can influence the behavior of entire populations simultaneously. What once required institutions, ideologies, or mass persuasion can now occur silently through optimization.

Importantly, humans adapt to decision-making environments. When systems reward certain behaviors—clicking, scrolling, responding quickly—people unconsciously adjust. The algorithm does not need to command; it nudges. Over time, these nudges accumulate into habits, preferences, and worldviews. In this way, AI does not merely assist decisions; it shapes the conditions under which decisions are made.

This does not mean that AI is inherently harmful or malicious. In many contexts, algorithmic decision-making improves accuracy, efficiency, and safety. The danger lies in uncritical delegation. When humans stop exercising judgment because machines appear more capable, the balance of intelligence shifts. Machines become authoritative not because they understand meaning, ethics, or consequence—but because they are faster, louder, and more consistent.

The move from tools to decision-makers represents a philosophical turning point. It forces humanity to confront a fundamental question: if machines increasingly decide what matters, what remains uniquely human? The answer will not be found in technology itself, but in how consciously humans choose to engage with it. The future of thinking machines depends not on their intelligence alone, but on whether human judgment remains active, vigilant, and indispensable.

How AI Quietly Entered Daily Life

Artificial Intelligence did not arrive with a dramatic takeover or a clear moment of transition. There was no single invention that signaled its dominance, no global announcement that human life was about to be shaped by algorithms. Instead, AI entered daily life quietly—through convenience, efficiency, and subtle delegation. Its influence grew not because people demanded it, but because they barely noticed it.

The earliest encounters with AI felt harmless. Spellcheck corrected mistakes. Search engines completed sentences. Photo apps enhanced images automatically. These systems did not present themselves as intelligent authorities; they appeared as helpful assistants designed to save time and reduce friction. Each interaction was small, almost trivial. Yet together, they formed the foundation of a new cognitive environment.

One of the key reasons AI integrated so seamlessly is that it aligned perfectly with modern human pressures. Life was already accelerating. People were overwhelmed by information, choices, and responsibilities. AI promised relief. It filtered options, ranked relevance, and predicted preferences. In a world of overload, reduction felt like liberation. Few questioned what was being reduced—or who decided what mattered.

Gradually, AI moved from background support to active participation. Navigation systems began choosing routes, not just displaying maps. Streaming platforms curated content instead of offering libraries. Online marketplaces highlighted products rather than letting users browse freely. Social media feeds stopped showing posts chronologically and started showing what algorithms deemed "engaging." Each shift replaced human exploration with machine selection.

This transition was subtle because it preserved the illusion of choice. Users still clicked, scrolled, and selected. But the options presented were already filtered. The boundaries of visibility narrowed. What appeared on the screen felt natural, even personalized, yet it was the result of continuous optimization. AI did not remove freedom outright; it redefined its shape.

Another factor that enabled AI's quiet entry was its invisibility. Unlike physical machines, algorithms have no presence. They operate silently, behind interfaces designed to feel intuitive and neutral. There is no visible moment when an algorithm intervenes. A recommendation feels like a suggestion, not a command. A ranking feels informative, not directive. This lack of friction reduces resistance.

Trust also played a critical role. AI systems were often introduced by familiar, reputable platforms. When technology comes wrapped in polished design and friendly language, skepticism diminishes. Over time, repeated accuracy reinforces confidence. When the system predicts correctly—what you want to watch, where traffic will clear, which email is spam—trust deepens. Trust, once established, invites dependence.

As AI embedded itself into routines, it became harder to imagine life without it. People stopped memorizing phone numbers, navigating by landmarks, or recalling facts. External systems handled memory, orientation, and recall. This outsourcing did not feel like loss; it felt like progress. Yet each relinquished task slightly weakened an internal cognitive skill.

AI also entered emotional and social spaces. Messaging apps suggested responses. Dating platforms ranked compatibility. Mental health chatbots offered support. Voice assistants responded conversationally. These systems blurred the line between tool and companion. Interaction became more human-like, even when understanding was simulated. The emotional comfort provided by responsiveness masked the absence of consciousness.

Crucially, AI's growth was driven by incentives that favored engagement over awareness. Systems were optimized to keep attention, increase usage, and influence behavior. The more seamlessly AI integrated, the more data it collected—and the more effective it became. This feedback loop accelerated adoption without requiring deliberate consent or reflection. Participation became automatic.

Education, work, and healthcare followed similar patterns. Automated grading tools, productivity software, diagnostic aids, and scheduling systems entered institutions as efficiency upgrades. Each reduced workload, but also reduced direct engagement. Teachers spent less time evaluating. Professionals followed system recommendations. Over time, human judgment shifted from primary to supervisory—approving decisions already shaped by algorithms.

The most striking aspect of AI's quiet arrival is how normalized it has become. Many people now experience reality through algorithmic mediation without recognizing it as such. What they see, hear, read, and consider is increasingly curated. AI does not dominate daily life through force or visibility, but through familiarity.

This quiet integration matters because influence is strongest when unnoticed. When people are unaware of guidance, they rarely question it. AI's power lies not in dramatic control, but in subtle shaping—of habits, expectations, and thought patterns. Understanding how AI entered daily life is essential, because only awareness creates the possibility of choice. Without awareness, influence feels like nature—and nature is rarely challenged.

When Assistance Became Authority

Artificial Intelligence did not begin as a ruler of decisions; it began as a helper. Early AI systems were framed as assistants—tools designed to support human judgment, not replace it. They corrected errors, organized information, and offered recommendations. Their role was explicitly secondary. Yet over time, the relationship between humans and machines subtly shifted. Assistance did not remain assistance. It evolved into authority.

This transformation occurred gradually, through repeated reliance rather than deliberate surrender. Each time an AI system produced a useful result, confidence increased. Each correct prediction reduced skepticism. As systems became more accurate, faster, and more consistent than humans in certain tasks, people began deferring to them—not because they were forced to, but because it felt reasonable. Trust turned into expectation.

One of the defining features of this shift is the framing of AI outputs. Algorithms rarely present their conclusions as commands. They appear as rankings, scores, probabilities, or "best options." This language preserves the appearance of human control while strongly guiding behavior. When a system labels something as "recommended," "optimized," or "high confidence," it implicitly defines what is sensible. To disagree feels irrational, even irresponsible.

Authority also emerges from asymmetry of information. AI systems process volumes of data no human can comprehend. This scale creates a psychological imbalance. When a machine draws conclusions from millions of data points, human intuition feels small and unreliable by comparison. The logic becomes circular: the system knows more, therefore it should decide; because it decides, it must know more.

Institutions accelerated this transition. In workplaces, AI-driven metrics began shaping performance evaluation. In finance, risk models influenced lending and investment. In healthcare, diagnostic tools guided clinical decisions. In law enforcement, predictive systems informed patrols and surveillance. Once organizations embed AI into workflows, individual discretion narrows. To challenge the system becomes to challenge institutional policy.

Crucially, responsibility did not increase alongside authority. When AI systems influence outcomes, humans often remain legally accountable, but psychologically distanced. Decisions are justified by pointing to the system: “the algorithm flagged it,” “the model predicted it,” “the system recommended it.” This diffusion of responsibility strengthens authority while weakening ethical ownership. Authority without accountability is a dangerous configuration.

The authority of AI is also reinforced by its consistency. Humans are variable. They tire, doubt, and contradict themselves. AI systems, by contrast, produce stable outputs. Stability is often mistaken for reliability. Over time, this leads to preference for machine judgment, even in situations involving nuance, context, or moral complexity. The system's confidence becomes persuasive, regardless of whether it understands meaning.

Another factor is habituation. When people repeatedly follow AI guidance, it becomes routine. The act of questioning fades. What was once a suggestion becomes the default path. Navigation apps illustrate this clearly: drivers stop evaluating routes and simply follow directions, even when intuition signals otherwise. The authority lies not in explicit control, but in habitual compliance.

This authority extends into perception itself. Algorithms decide what news appears, which voices are amplified, and what narratives dominate attention. Over time, exposure shapes belief. The system does not tell users what to think; it decides what they encounter. Authority over visibility becomes authority over thought. When reality is filtered, interpretation follows.

Importantly, AI authority is not experienced as oppression. It feels efficient, helpful, even comforting. People are relieved to outsource decisions in a complex world. Cognitive effort is reduced. Uncertainty feels managed. Yet this comfort comes at a cost: diminished agency. When decision-making muscles are unused, they weaken. Judgment atrophies through disuse.

The danger is not that AI becomes powerful, but that humans become passive. Authority shifts quietly when people stop insisting on participation. Machines do not demand control; they accept what is given. The transition from assistance to authority is enabled by human convenience, trust, and fatigue.

Recognizing this shift is essential. Authority should emerge from wisdom, accountability, and ethical responsibility—not from speed or scale alone. Artificial Intelligence can support human judgment, but it cannot replace moral reasoning, contextual understanding, or lived experience. When assistance becomes authority without scrutiny, human agency erodes.

The future relationship between humans and AI depends on whether this authority is examined, limited, and shared—or allowed to grow unchecked. True intelligence, after all, is not merely the ability to decide, but the responsibility to understand the consequences of those decisions.

Chapter 2:
The Outsourcing of Human Thinking

Human thinking has never existed in isolation. Throughout history, tools, traditions, and social structures have shaped how people reason and decide. Yet even within these influences, judgment remained a distinctly human act—slow, effortful, and rooted in personal responsibility. Artificial Intelligence introduces a new condition: thinking itself is no longer merely supported by tools; it is increasingly outsourced to them.

This chapter explores how judgment, once cultivated through experience and reflection, is now frequently automated. AI systems assess risk, rank relevance, predict behavior, and recommend action at a scale and speed no individual can match. In many environments, these systems are no longer optional aids; they define workflows, expectations, and outcomes. Humans do not so much decide as approve what has already been decided.

The appeal of this shift is obvious. Automation reduces effort. It promises consistency, efficiency, and relief from cognitive overload. In a world saturated with information and choice, surrendering judgment can feel rational. Convenience, however, is not neutral. When thinking becomes effortless, it also becomes shallow. The mind adapts to reduced demand, and skills once exercised regularly begin to weaken.

As reliance on automated judgment increases, independent reasoning declines—not because humans lose intelligence, but because they use it less. People learn to trust outputs over processes, answers over understanding. The question "why" is replaced by "what does the system say?" Over time, critical thinking is reframed as inefficiency, and hesitation is mistaken for incompetence.

This chapter examines the psychological, cultural, and cognitive consequences of outsourcing thought. It asks what happens when mental effort is systematically minimized and when machines become the default arbiters of correctness. More importantly, it challenges the assumption that efficiency is always a virtue.

The outsourcing of human thinking does not occur through coercion. It happens through convenience. Understanding this shift is essential, because once judgment is surrendered, reclaiming it becomes increasingly difficult.

Automation of Judgment

Judgment has always been one of the defining features of human intelligence. It involves weighing evidence, interpreting context, balancing competing values, and accepting responsibility for outcomes. Unlike calculation, judgment is not purely mechanical; it is shaped by experience, intuition, moral reasoning, and awareness of uncertainty. The automation of judgment marks a profound shift, because it transfers this deeply human function to systems that do not understand meaning, consequence, or responsibility.

Artificial Intelligence automates judgment by translating complex human decisions into data-driven processes. Behaviors are quantified, preferences are inferred, risks are scored, and outcomes are predicted. What once required deliberation is now reduced to probabilities and rankings. In theory, this promises objectivity. In practice, it reshapes how decisions are made and who is considered authoritative.

One of the earliest domains to adopt automated judgment was finance. Credit scores, fraud detection systems, and algorithmic trading models began determining access to capital and opportunity. These systems assess trustworthiness based on historical patterns, not personal circumstance. A numerical score replaces a holistic evaluation. For individuals, the judgment feels impersonal and opaque, yet difficult to challenge. The decision exists, but the reasoning is inaccessible.

Healthcare followed a similar path. Diagnostic algorithms now analyze medical images, symptoms, and patient histories to recommend treatments. While these tools can improve accuracy, they also alter clinical judgment. Physicians increasingly consult systems before forming conclusions. Over time, professional intuition becomes secondary. When the machine contradicts the human, the burden of proof shifts. The algorithm's recommendation often carries more weight than lived expertise.

Automation of judgment thrives in environments where speed and scale are prioritized. In hiring, AI filters résumés before a human sees them. In education, automated grading systems assess performance. In law enforcement, predictive models estimate risk and allocate resources. These systems are efficient, but efficiency narrows perspective. What cannot be measured is often ignored. Context is flattened. Nuance is lost.

The psychological effect of automated judgment is subtle but significant. When people encounter decisions made by machines, they are more likely to accept them without question. This phenomenon, sometimes called "automation bias," reflects a tendency to over-trust system outputs. Humans assume that because the system is advanced, it must be correct. Doubt feels irrational, even when evidence suggests otherwise.

This bias intensifies with repetition. The more often a system delivers acceptable results, the more its authority solidifies. Humans begin to defer automatically. Judgment becomes reactive rather than proactive. Instead of forming an independent conclusion and checking it against the system, people wait for the system's output and align their thinking accordingly. The direction of reasoning reverses.

Automation also changes how responsibility is perceived. When judgment is delegated to a system, accountability becomes blurred. Individuals feel less personally responsible for outcomes. A rejected application, a denied claim, or a flagged risk can be attributed to "the system." This diffusion of responsibility reduces moral engagement. Decisions feel inevitable rather than chosen.

Importantly, automated judgment is not neutral. AI systems learn from data generated by human behavior and institutional practices. If those practices contain bias, inequality, or flawed assumptions, the system encodes and amplifies them. Yet because the output appears objective, its conclusions are often treated as fair. Bias becomes harder to see when it is hidden behind complexity.

Another consequence is the narrowing of acceptable reasoning. Automated systems define norms. What the system predicts becomes what is expected. Outliers are treated as errors rather than signals. Human judgment, which often thrives on anomaly and contradiction, is pressured to conform. Creativity, dissent, and ethical hesitation are seen as inefficiencies in a system optimized for consistency.

The automation of judgment also affects how individuals view themselves. When machines assess performance, risk, or value, people internalize these evaluations. A score becomes an identity. Self-worth is quantified. The human experience is reduced to metrics. Over time, individuals may begin to see themselves through the lens of algorithmic assessment, adjusting behavior to satisfy the system rather than personal values.

Despite these risks, automation of judgment is not inherently harmful. In high-stakes environments, well-designed systems can reduce error and support human decision-making. The danger lies in replacement rather than collaboration. Judgment should be augmented, not surrendered.

To preserve human agency, automated judgment must remain transparent, contestable, and subordinate to human responsibility. Systems can inform, but humans must decide. Judgment, after all, is not merely about choosing efficiently—it is about understanding consequences, bearing responsibility, and acting with wisdom. When that function is automated without restraint, something essential is lost.

Convenience vs. Cognitive Effort

Human thinking has always required effort. Reflection, problem-solving, memory, and judgment demand time, focus, and mental energy. Throughout history, cognitive effort was unavoidable because tools could only assist, not replace, thinking. Artificial Intelligence alters this balance by offering unprecedented convenience—instant answers, automated decisions, and frictionless experiences. While this convenience appears beneficial, it introduces a trade-off that is rarely examined: the gradual erosion of cognitive effort.

Convenience is seductive because it promises relief from mental strain. In a fast-paced world filled with constant demands, reducing effort feels like progress. AI systems search, summarize, recommend, and decide within seconds. They eliminate uncertainty and compress complexity into manageable outputs. What once required exploration now requires a click. Over time, the brain adapts to this lowered demand.

Cognitive effort functions like a muscle. When it is exercised, it strengthens; when it is avoided, it weakens. Skills such as critical thinking, deep focus, and memory depend on repeated use. AI-driven convenience reduces the need for these skills. Navigation apps replace spatial reasoning. Search engines replace recall. Recommendation systems replace curiosity. Each substitution appears minor, but their cumulative effect is significant.

The shift from effort to ease changes how people approach problems. Instead of engaging deeply, individuals learn to expect immediate solutions. Patience declines. Tolerance for ambiguity diminishes. When answers are not instant, frustration increases. This psychological shift alters expectations about thinking itself. Effort begins to feel inefficient rather than necessary.

Education illustrates this tension clearly. Learning traditionally involved struggle—working through confusion, making mistakes, and synthesizing understanding. AI tools now provide instant explanations, summaries, and solutions. While helpful, they risk bypassing the cognitive processes that lead to comprehension. Students may achieve correct answers without understanding the underlying logic. Effort is replaced by output, and learning becomes superficial.

Convenience also reshapes attention. AI systems are designed to minimize friction, presenting information in easily consumable forms. Short summaries replace long texts. Highlights replace full arguments. Visual cues replace sustained reading. Attention fragments as systems compete to retain engagement. Deep thinking, which requires sustained effort, becomes increasingly rare.

Importantly, convenience is not evenly distributed across cognitive domains. AI optimizes for efficiency, not wisdom. It reduces effort in areas that require reflection, but not in areas that demand compliance. Users still expend effort scrolling, clicking, and responding—effort directed toward engagement rather than understanding. The brain remains active, but not thoughtful.

Another consequence of reduced cognitive effort is overconfidence. When systems provide polished outputs, users may mistake ease for mastery. The illusion of understanding replaces genuine comprehension.

People feel informed because information is accessible, not because it has been processed. This creates shallow knowledge—broad but fragile, easily disrupted by complexity.

Convenience also affects decision-making. When AI systems present "best options," individuals are spared the effort of evaluation. Over time, this reduces confidence in personal judgment. Choosing becomes an act of selection among recommendations rather than a process of reasoning. The mind shifts from active deliberation to passive acceptance.

The long-term risk is cognitive dependency. When effort is consistently outsourced, regaining it becomes difficult. Tasks that once felt manageable begin to feel taxing. Independent thinking requires stamina, and stamina declines without practice. The convenience that once felt empowering becomes constraining.

This does not mean that convenience is inherently harmful. Reducing unnecessary cognitive load can free mental resources for creativity, empathy, and insight. The problem arises when convenience replaces effort rather than reallocating it. When thinking is minimized rather than redirected, the human mind adapts downward.

A healthy relationship with AI requires intentional friction. Some effort is essential for growth. Struggle is not a flaw in human cognition; it is a feature. It forces engagement, builds understanding, and strengthens judgment. Convenience should serve human thinking, not replace it.

The tension between convenience and cognitive effort defines the modern intellectual environment. As AI continues to streamline experience, humans must decide what they are willing to lose in exchange for ease. The true cost of convenience is not measured in time saved, but in thinking surrendered.

The Decline of Independent Reasoning

Independent reasoning is the capacity to form conclusions through personal analysis rather than external direction. It involves questioning assumptions, evaluating evidence, tolerating uncertainty, and accepting responsibility for one's judgments. This capacity has long been considered a hallmark of human intelligence and autonomy. In the age of

Artificial Intelligence, however, independent reasoning is not forcibly removed—it quietly recedes.

The decline does not begin with ignorance, but with reliance. AI systems offer recommendations, predictions, and answers with remarkable speed and confidence. When these outputs consistently appear accurate, humans naturally begin to trust them. Trust, repeated often enough, becomes default behavior. Instead of reasoning first and verifying later, people increasingly wait for algorithmic guidance before forming opinions.

One of the most significant drivers of this shift is cognitive offloading. Humans have always offloaded tasks—writing replaced memorization, maps replaced mental navigation. AI accelerates this process by offloading judgment itself. When systems assess credibility, relevance, or risk, individuals no longer practice those evaluations. Over time, unused cognitive skills weaken. The ability to reason independently declines through disuse, not incapacity.

Information environments play a critical role. Algorithms curate what people see, shaping perception before reasoning even begins. News feeds, search results, and recommendations define the boundaries of awareness. When exposure is filtered, reasoning is constrained. People reason within the options presented, rarely questioning what is absent. Independent thought becomes bounded by algorithmic visibility.

Social reinforcement further accelerates the decline. AI-driven platforms optimize for engagement, amplifying content that aligns with existing beliefs. This creates echo chambers where ideas are reinforced rather than challenged. Independent reasoning thrives on friction—on encountering opposing views and resolving tension. When friction is removed, thought becomes passive and reactive.

The decline is also psychological. Independent reasoning requires effort, and effort carries risk. One might be wrong, misunderstood, or challenged. AI offers certainty without vulnerability. Following recommendations feels safer than standing alone. Over time, individuals may lose confidence in their own judgment, deferring to systems even in matters of personal values.

Education systems are not immune. When students rely on AI-generated explanations or answers, they may achieve outcomes without developing reasoning processes. Assessment shifts from understanding to performance. The habit of working through uncertainty weakens. Independent reasoning, which depends on struggle and reflection, is replaced by efficient output.

In professional settings, algorithmic guidance shapes decisions. Metrics, dashboards, and predictive models define success. Employees learn to align with system outputs rather than question them. Dissent becomes inefficiency. Independent reasoning is discouraged not explicitly, but structurally. When systems reward compliance, reasoning adapts accordingly.

Importantly, the decline of independent reasoning is not uniform. It affects domains differently. Technical tasks may benefit from automation, while ethical, creative, and strategic reasoning suffer. AI excels at pattern recognition, not meaning-making. When humans rely on it in areas requiring judgment, reasoning narrows.

Another subtle effect is the erosion of curiosity. Independent reasoning begins with questions. When answers are immediate and abundant, curiosity diminishes. The habit of inquiry fades. Instead of asking "why," individuals ask "what does the system say?" The direction of thought shifts outward.

The long-term consequences extend beyond individual cognition. A society with diminished independent reasoning becomes more susceptible to manipulation. When people rely on external systems to define truth, authority consolidates. Critical thinking weakens. Democratic deliberation suffers. The capacity to challenge narratives declines.

Yet this decline is not inevitable. Independent reasoning can be preserved through intentional practice. It requires awareness of when systems guide thought and a willingness to resist convenience. It requires education that values process over output and cultures that reward questioning rather than conformity.

Artificial Intelligence can support reasoning by providing information and insight, but it cannot replace the human responsibility to think.

Independent reasoning is not obsolete; it is endangered. Its preservation depends on conscious choice.

The future of intelligence will not be determined solely by technological capability, but by whether humans continue to reason independently in a world increasingly eager to think for them.

Chapter 3:
Attention in the Age of Algorithms

Attention is the gateway to thought. What the mind attends to determines what it remembers, understands, and values. For most of human history, attention was shaped by environment, necessity, and personal intention. In the digital age, attention has become a resource—measured, optimized, and monetized. Artificial Intelligence sits at the center of this transformation, quietly governing what captures focus and what fades into the background.

This chapter examines how algorithms have assumed unprecedented control over human attention. AI-driven systems do not merely respond to user interest; they actively shape it. By analyzing behavior in real time, algorithms predict what will hold attention longest and adjust content accordingly. What appears spontaneous is carefully optimized. Focus becomes guided rather than chosen.

As attention is continuously fragmented by algorithmic design, its natural duration shortens. Sustained focus—once essential for reading, learning, and reflection—becomes increasingly difficult. The mind adapts to rapid stimulation, preferring novelty over depth. Pauses feel uncomfortable. Silence feels empty. This shift alters not only how long people pay attention, but how they experience thinking itself.

At the neurological level, algorithms exploit reward mechanisms. Endless feeds, notifications, and variable reinforcement stimulate dopamine responses that keep users engaged. Scrolling becomes habitual rather than intentional. Engagement is sustained not by meaning, but by anticipation. The brain learns to seek constant input, reducing tolerance for stillness and concentration.

This chapter explores the consequences of algorithmic attention control on cognition, creativity, and emotional well-being. It asks what happens when focus is no longer self-directed, and when the mind is trained to respond rather than reflect. Understanding attention in the age of algorithms is essential, because whoever controls attention ultimately shapes thought—and thought shapes reality.

Algorithmic Control of Focus

Attention has become one of the most valuable resources of the modern age. In a world saturated with information, the ability to direct focus determines what people learn, believe, and remember. Artificial Intelligence now plays a central role in this process. Through continuous analysis of behavior, algorithms increasingly control not only what captures attention, but how long it is held and in what sequence it unfolds.

Algorithmic control of focus operates through personalization. AI systems monitor clicks, pauses, scrolling speed, reactions, and dwell time. From these signals, they infer interest, emotion, and intent. Content is then adjusted in real time to maximize engagement. What the user sees next is not random; it is optimized. The result is an experience that feels tailored, yet is designed to keep attention captive.

This control is subtle because it preserves the appearance of choice. Users select content, but the menu itself is algorithmically curated. Visibility becomes power. Items that align with predicted engagement rise; others disappear. Over time, the algorithm defines relevance. Focus narrows around what the system amplifies. Awareness of alternatives fades.

The structure of digital platforms reinforces this dynamic. Infinite feeds eliminate natural stopping points. Autoplay removes decision-making. Notifications interrupt concentration. These features are not accidental; they are optimized outcomes of algorithmic learning. The system experiments constantly, refining what sustains focus longest. Human attention becomes a variable to be tuned.

Importantly, algorithmic focus is not neutral. It prioritizes content that provokes strong emotional responses—outrage, fear, excitement—because such responses prolong engagement. Nuanced, reflective material is disadvantaged. This skews the informational environment, favoring immediacy over depth. Focus becomes reactive rather than deliberate.

As algorithms shape focus, they also shape perception. When attention is repeatedly drawn to specific themes or narratives, those elements feel more significant. The mind confuses frequency with importance. What appears often seems relevant; what appears rarely seems trivial. This distortion influences beliefs without explicit persuasion.

Algorithmic control also fragments attention. By presenting multiple stimuli in rapid succession, systems train the mind to shift focus frequently. Sustained concentration becomes difficult. The brain adapts to novelty and speed. This adaptation is not benign. It alters cognitive rhythms, reducing the capacity for deep work and contemplation.

The economic incentives behind algorithmic focus intensify its impact. Attention drives revenue. Platforms are rewarded for keeping users engaged, not for fostering understanding. AI systems optimize for measurable outcomes, not intangible qualities like wisdom or insight. Focus is captured, not cultivated.

This control extends beyond entertainment. News, education, and social interaction are mediated by algorithms. What topics trend, what voices are amplified, and what discussions persist are influenced by engagement metrics. Public discourse becomes shaped by what holds attention, not by what matters most.

Crucially, algorithmic control of focus reduces self-awareness. When attention is guided externally, individuals may lose the habit of directing it intentionally. The question "What should I focus on?" is replaced by "What is being shown?" Over time, agency diminishes.

Recognizing algorithmic control is the first step toward reclaiming attention. Focus is not merely a cognitive function; it is a moral one. Where attention goes, energy follows. Where energy flows, values form. In an age of intelligent systems, preserving the ability to choose what deserves focus is essential to preserving human autonomy.

The challenge is not to eliminate algorithms, but to resist surrendering attention entirely. Awareness creates friction. Friction creates choice. And choice restores control in a landscape increasingly designed to decide for us.

Shortened Attention Spans

The shortening of human attention spans is one of the most visible cognitive shifts of the AI-driven age. What once felt natural—reading for long periods, listening without interruption, thinking deeply—now often feels demanding or even uncomfortable. This change did not occur because human intelligence declined, but because the environment in which attention operates has been fundamentally redesigned.

Artificial Intelligence systems are optimized for speed, novelty, and engagement. They deliver information in rapid bursts, constantly refreshing content to capture interest. Over time, the brain adapts to this rhythm. Attention becomes trained for quick stimulation rather than sustained focus. The result is not an inability to pay attention, but a reconditioning of how attention functions.

Human attention evolved in environments that rewarded patience. Hunting, learning, craftsmanship, storytelling, and problem-solving all required extended concentration. Modern algorithmic environments reward the opposite. Content is optimized to be immediately engaging, easily digestible, and quickly replaced. When focus is no longer required for survival or success, it weakens through disuse.

Shortened attention spans are not caused by distraction alone, but by expectation. When the mind becomes accustomed to constant novelty, it begins to expect it. Slow processes feel inefficient. Long explanations feel excessive. Silence feels empty. This expectation reshapes cognition. The brain seeks stimulation more frequently, reducing tolerance for sustained effort.

AI-driven platforms accelerate this process through continuous feedback. Each scroll, click, or swipe delivers a small reward. These micro-rewards reinforce brief engagement cycles. Attention is fragmented into moments rather than sustained states. The mind learns to reset focus repeatedly instead of maintaining it.

This fragmentation has consequences for learning and comprehension. Deep understanding requires holding ideas in mind, connecting concepts, and reflecting on meaning. When attention is brief, processing becomes shallow. Information is consumed, but not integrated. Knowledge becomes surface-level—recognized rather than understood.

Reading habits illustrate this change clearly. Long-form reading demands sustained focus, yet many people now skim rather than read. Headlines replace arguments. Summaries replace analysis. AI systems further reinforce this trend by prioritizing concise, high-engagement formats. The skill of deep reading declines not because it is obsolete, but because it is rarely practiced.

Shortened attention spans also affect emotional regulation. Sustained attention helps individuals process emotions, reflect on experiences, and build resilience. When attention is constantly redirected, emotional processing is interrupted. Feelings are reacted to rather than understood. This contributes to anxiety, restlessness, and reduced emotional depth.

Importantly, shortened attention does not mean reduced intelligence. Humans remain capable of focus when required. The issue is that the environment rarely requires it. When attention is constantly captured externally, the internal discipline to sustain it weakens. Like any skill, attention requires deliberate practice.

Education systems face growing challenges as a result. Students raised in algorithmic environments may struggle with tasks requiring extended focus. This is not a failure of ability, but a mismatch between cognitive conditioning and educational demands. When learning environments do not adapt thoughtfully, frustration increases on both sides.

The workplace is similarly affected. Complex problem-solving requires sustained attention. Yet constant notifications, automated alerts, and multitasking expectations fragment focus. Productivity becomes measured by responsiveness rather than depth. AI tools that promise efficiency can inadvertently undermine the concentration needed for meaningful work.

The cultural impact is equally significant. Public discourse becomes simplified. Nuanced arguments struggle to compete with emotionally charged fragments. Attention favors immediacy over reflection. As a result, complex issues are reduced to slogans, and thoughtful dialogue gives way to rapid reaction.

Shortened attention spans also influence self-perception. When individuals struggle to concentrate, they may interpret it as personal weakness rather than environmental conditioning. This misunderstanding leads to self-blame rather than systemic awareness. The problem is not the mind—it is the context in which the mind operates.

Reversing this trend requires intentional resistance. Attention must be treated as a finite resource worth protecting. This does not mean rejecting AI, but using it consciously. Systems should serve human goals, not redefine them.

Sustained attention remains essential for creativity, wisdom, and self-understanding. In an age of algorithms, preserving this capacity is not automatic—it is a choice. The length of human attention may be shrinking, but its value has never been greater.

Dopamine, Feeds, and Endless Scrolling

At the core of endless scrolling lies a simple neurological mechanism: dopamine. Dopamine is not the chemical of pleasure, as it is often misunderstood, but the chemical of anticipation. It motivates seeking behavior—the urge to check, to look again, to continue. Artificial Intelligence–driven platforms are engineered to exploit this mechanism with remarkable precision, transforming attention into habit and habit into dependency.

Endless feeds are not accidental design choices. They are the product of continuous algorithmic experimentation. AI systems test what keeps users engaged longest, adjusting content delivery in real time. Variable rewards—unpredictable likes, surprising posts, unexpected information—trigger dopamine responses similar to those observed in gambling. The user does not scroll because they are satisfied, but because they are expecting something better to appear next.

This anticipation loop is powerful because it bypasses conscious intention. Unlike deliberate activities, scrolling often begins reflexively. A moment of boredom, discomfort, or silence prompts a check. One swipe becomes another. The feed has no natural stopping point, removing the cognitive cue to disengage. Without closure, attention drifts forward indefinitely.

Dopamine-driven engagement reshapes the brain's reward system.

When stimulation is constant, baseline dopamine sensitivity decreases. Activities that once felt rewarding—reading, conversation, reflection—begin to feel dull by comparison. The mind seeks higher-frequency input to achieve the same level of engagement. This escalation fuels longer scrolling sessions and shorter tolerance for slower experiences.

AI systems intensify this effect by personalizing feeds. Content is selected not only for relevance, but for emotional impact. Posts that provoke outrage, excitement, or validation generate stronger engagement signals. Over time, the feed becomes optimized for emotional spikes rather than informational value. The brain learns to associate scrolling with emotional stimulation, reinforcing the habit.

This dynamic blurs the line between choice and compulsion. Users believe they are freely engaging, yet their behavior is being shaped by invisible reinforcement schedules. The more one scrolls, the more data the system gathers, and the better it becomes at sustaining engagement. This feedback loop strengthens over time, making disengagement increasingly difficult.

Endless scrolling also fragments time perception. Short bursts of engagement accumulate unnoticed. Minutes turn into hours. Because each interaction feels brief, the overall duration is underestimated. This distortion contributes to a sense of time scarcity and mental fatigue. The mind is occupied, yet unsatisfied.

The cognitive consequences are significant. Continuous dopamine stimulation reduces the brain's capacity for sustained focus. When reward is immediate and frequent, patience declines. Tasks requiring delayed gratification feel burdensome. Creativity, which often emerges from boredom and reflection, is suppressed. Silence becomes something to escape rather than explore.

Emotionally, endless scrolling fosters volatility. Rapid exposure to varied content—humor, tragedy, outrage, validation—creates emotional whiplash. The nervous system is constantly activated but rarely settled. This contributes to anxiety, irritability, and restlessness. Emotional depth gives way to emotional reactivity.

AI-driven feeds also affect self-perception. Social comparison is amplified. Metrics such as likes, views, and shares become proxies for value. Dopamine rewards reinforce behaviors that align with platform incentives rather than personal authenticity. Identity becomes performative, shaped by what receives attention.

Importantly, dopamine itself is not harmful. It is essential for motivation and learning. The issue lies in artificial amplification. When systems are designed to maximize dopamine triggers, they hijack natural reward pathways. Engagement becomes the goal rather than a byproduct. The human brain, evolved for environments of scarcity, struggles to regulate abundance.

The normalization of endless scrolling masks its impact. Because the behavior is widespread, it feels harmless. Yet its effects accumulate quietly. Attention shortens. Reflection diminishes. Presence erodes. The mind becomes accustomed to constant input, reducing tolerance for stillness.

Breaking this cycle requires awareness. Understanding that feeds are engineered—not neutral—restores agency. Small interventions, such as intentional pauses, defined endpoints, and mindful use, can reintroduce control. The goal is not abstinence, but balance.

In the age of AI, dopamine is no longer merely a biological function; it is a target. Endless scrolling thrives on anticipation, not fulfillment. Reclaiming attention means recognizing when stimulation replaces meaning—and choosing depth over endless motion.

Chapter 4:
Memory, Knowledge, and Intellectual Dependency

Memory has always been central to human intelligence. It allows individuals to learn from experience, build understanding over time, and develop wisdom through reflection. Knowledge, once internalized, shaped judgment and identity. In the age of Artificial Intelligence, this relationship is undergoing a quiet transformation. Memory is no longer primarily something we cultivate; it is something we access.

This chapter explores how AI-driven systems are reshaping the way humans remember, know, and understand. Search engines, cloud storage, recommendation systems, and intelligent assistants have become external repositories of information. Facts, directions, explanations, and even personal memories are increasingly stored outside the mind. The result is not simply improved access to knowledge, but a growing dependency on retrieval rather than retention.

Remembering less is not inherently problematic. Writing and printing once transformed memory in similar ways. What distinguishes the current shift is scale, speed, and intimacy. AI systems do not merely store information; they decide what is surfaced, when, and how. Knowledge is not just available—it is curated, summarized, and ranked. This changes how people relate to information itself.

As reliance on external systems grows, internal memory adapts. When information is always retrievable, the incentive to remember weakens. Cognitive effort shifts from understanding to searching. Familiarity replaces mastery. Individuals know where to find answers, but not necessarily how to evaluate them. Intellectual confidence becomes tied to access rather than comprehension.

This chapter examines the consequences of treating AI as an external brain. It asks what happens when recall is outsourced and when knowledge is experienced as transient rather than internalized. More importantly, it explores how intellectual dependency shapes reasoning, creativity, and autonomy.

The central concern is not memory loss, but memory displacement. When the mind relies on systems to remember, the nature of knowledge itself changes. Understanding this shift is essential, because memory is not merely storage—it is the foundation of thought.

Remembering Less, Searching More

Human memory has never been static. Throughout history, methods of storing and transmitting knowledge have evolved, from oral tradition to writing, from books to digital archives. Each shift changed how people remembered, but none altered the relationship between memory and thinking as radically as Artificial Intelligence. Today, remembering is no longer the primary pathway to knowing. Searching has taken its place.

In an AI-driven world, information is always available. Facts, definitions, instructions, and explanations can be retrieved instantly. This constant accessibility changes how the mind allocates effort. When answers are guaranteed, remembering feels unnecessary. The brain adapts by conserving energy, prioritizing retrieval strategies over retention. Instead of committing knowledge to memory, individuals remember how to find it.

This shift may appear efficient, but it has deeper cognitive consequences. Memory is not merely a storage system; it is an active process that shapes understanding. Remembering requires engagement, repetition, and context. When information is internalized, it becomes part of a mental framework that supports reasoning, creativity, and insight. Searching, by contrast, delivers isolated fragments. It provides answers without integration.

Artificial Intelligence accelerates this trend by reducing friction in retrieval. Search engines anticipate queries. Assistants respond conversationally. Algorithms summarize content. The effort required to access information approaches zero. When effort disappears, so does the incentive to remember. The mind learns that storing knowledge internally is inefficient compared to outsourcing it.

Over time, this alters how people perceive knowledge itself. Knowing becomes synonymous with access. Confidence comes from connectivity rather than comprehension. Individuals may feel informed because information is available, even if it has not been processed deeply. This creates a form of intellectual shallowness—broad awareness without depth.

The impact is particularly visible in everyday cognition. People struggle to recall phone numbers, directions, dates, or basic facts that were once memorized. This is not a sign of declining intelligence, but of changing cognitive priorities. Memory adapts to environment. When the environment guarantees retrieval, memory reallocates its resources elsewhere.

However, this reallocation comes at a cost. Internal memory supports pattern recognition, critical thinking, and synthesis. When knowledge resides within the mind, connections form naturally. Ideas build on one another. Insight emerges from recombination. When knowledge is external, these processes weaken. Each search begins anew, disconnected from prior understanding.

Searching also changes how questions are framed. Instead of exploring a problem, individuals seek immediate answers. The question becomes transactional: "What is the answer?" rather than exploratory: "How does this work?" This mindset discourages curiosity and reflection. The journey of understanding is replaced by destination-based thinking.

AI-driven search systems further shape this behavior by optimizing for speed and relevance rather than depth. Results are ranked, summarized, and simplified. Complexity is compressed. While this improves usability, it also reduces exposure to nuance. The user receives an answer, not an argument. Memory, which thrives on complexity and repetition, is bypassed.

Educational contexts reveal the long-term implications. Students raised in environments of instant retrieval may struggle to retain foundational knowledge. They learn to search rather than to remember. While this enables quick performance, it undermines long-term mastery. Without internalized knowledge, higher-order thinking becomes difficult. One cannot critically evaluate what one does not understand.

Professional life is similarly affected. Expertise depends on accumulated knowledge and experience. When professionals rely heavily on search and AI tools, their internal knowledge base may stagnate. Decision-making becomes reactive, guided by external inputs rather than internal judgment. Over time, confidence in personal expertise erodes.

Importantly, remembering less is not inherently harmful. External memory systems can free cognitive resources for creativity and problem-solving. The danger lies in imbalance. When searching replaces remembering entirely, the mind becomes dependent. Dependency reduces resilience. When systems fail, understanding falters.

There is also an ethical dimension. When knowledge is accessed through AI systems, it is mediated. Algorithms decide what appears, what is emphasized, and what is omitted. When individuals rely on search rather than memory, they also rely on these filters. Intellectual independence weakens as knowledge pathways narrow.

The shift from remembering to searching is not a flaw of technology, but a predictable adaptation. The question is not whether humans will search more, but whether they will remember enough. Memory is not obsolete; it is foundational. It enables meaning, context, and continuity.

Preserving memory in the age of AI requires intentional practice. It requires choosing to learn deeply rather than retrieve endlessly. Searching can support memory, but it cannot replace it. When humans stop remembering, they do not just forget facts—they lose the structure that makes thinking possible.

External Brains and Digital Recall

The human brain evolved to remember, interpret, and connect experiences across time. Memory was once inseparable from identity, knowledge, and judgment. In the age of Artificial Intelligence, this relationship has changed. Increasingly, humans rely on external systems to store, organize, and retrieve information. These systems function as "external brains," reshaping how memory operates and how knowledge is experienced.

Digital recall differs fundamentally from human memory. Human memory is associative, emotional, and imperfect. It filters experience, emphasizing meaning over precision. Digital systems, by contrast, are exact, searchable, and limitless. They store information without context or feeling. When humans rely on digital recall, they trade richness for accuracy and accessibility.

AI-driven tools amplify this shift. Intelligent assistants remember appointments, preferences, and conversations. Cloud services archive photos, messages, and documents. Search engines retrieve facts instantly. These systems relieve cognitive burden, allowing individuals to function efficiently in complex environments. However, efficiency comes with a subtle cost: diminished engagement with memory itself.

External brains change how people interact with information. Instead of remembering, individuals learn to rely on prompts. Notifications replace recall. Reminders replace planning. The mind becomes reactive, responding to signals rather than actively holding information. This alters cognitive habits. Memory becomes something triggered rather than sustained.

This dependency affects not only factual recall, but personal experience. Digital archives store moments that were once remembered through reflection. Photos replace recollection. Timelines replace narrative. Memory becomes fragmented, outsourced to platforms that organize life into searchable units. The personal past becomes a database rather than a story.

The presence of external brains also influences learning. When information is always retrievable, the motivation to internalize it weakens. Students may focus on accessing resources rather than mastering content. Understanding becomes shallow. Knowledge exists externally, disconnected from internal frameworks that support reasoning and creativity.

AI systems further mediate digital recall by deciding what is surfaced. Algorithms prioritize relevance based on past behavior. Memory becomes curated. What is recalled is not neutral, but optimized. Over time, this shapes perception. Certain information feels more salient because it is repeatedly presented, while other knowledge fades into obscurity.

External brains also alter trust. When digital systems remember accurately, humans may begin to distrust their own memory. Doubt arises: "Did this happen the way I recall?" The system's record feels authoritative. Personal memory, with its imperfections, feels unreliable. This undermines confidence in subjective experience.

Another consequence is the erosion of cognitive resilience. Human memory adapts to challenge. When recall requires effort, neural pathways strengthen. External brains remove this effort. Over time, recall skills weaken. Tasks that once required memory now require access. When access is disrupted, functioning falters.

The reliance on external brains also raises ethical concerns. Data stored externally is controlled by institutions. Access can be restricted, altered, or monetized. When memory resides outside the individual, autonomy is reduced. Intellectual independence becomes contingent on systems beyond personal control.

Despite these risks, external brains are not inherently harmful. They extend human capability and preserve information beyond natural limits. The danger lies in overreliance. When digital recall replaces internal memory entirely, the balance shifts. Memory is not merely storage; it is the foundation of understanding.

Human memory integrates emotion, context, and meaning. It supports identity and continuity. Digital recall cannot replicate these qualities. It retrieves data, not experience. When humans confuse retrieval with understanding, knowledge becomes shallow.

Preserving a healthy relationship with external brains requires intentional boundaries. Digital systems should support memory, not replace it. They should assist recall, not define it. Humans must choose what to internalize and what to outsource.

The rise of external brains challenges humanity to reconsider what it means to know. Knowledge is not merely accessible information; it is internalized understanding. In an age of AI, remembering remains essential—not despite technology, but because of it.

What Happens When Knowledge Is Always Retrieved

When knowledge is always retrievable, the relationship between humans and understanding changes in fundamental ways. Artificial Intelligence has transformed information access from an effortful process into an instant response. Answers appear on demand, often before questions are fully formed. While this convenience feels empowering, it reshapes how knowledge is valued, processed, and integrated into thought.

Retrieval replaces retention when access is guaranteed. The brain, designed to conserve energy, adapts to this environment. If information can be retrieved instantly, there is little incentive to store it internally. Memory becomes externalized. Knowing shifts from internal comprehension to external availability. This transformation alters not just what people know, but how they think.

Knowledge that is always retrieved tends to remain superficial. Internalized knowledge forms networks of understanding, allowing ideas to connect and evolve. Retrieved knowledge arrives as isolated fragments. Each query produces a result, but not necessarily a framework. Without internal structures, information remains detached. Insight, which depends on synthesis, becomes harder to achieve.

Constant retrieval also weakens judgment. When individuals rely on systems to supply answers, they practice less evaluation. The habit of questioning sources, weighing evidence, and reflecting on implications declines. Answers feel authoritative because they are immediate. Speed substitutes for reliability. The process of reasoning is bypassed.

AI systems further shape this dynamic by curating responses. Algorithms decide which answers are presented, how they are framed, and what context is included. Knowledge becomes mediated. When retrieval is filtered, understanding is shaped by invisible criteria. The user receives what is optimized, not necessarily what is comprehensive or truthful.

This environment encourages intellectual passivity. Instead of engaging with complexity, individuals consume outputs. Curiosity becomes transactional. Questions are asked to obtain answers, not to explore ideas. Over time, the joy of discovery diminishes. Learning becomes a means to an end rather than a process of growth.

Education illustrates these consequences clearly. Students accustomed to constant retrieval may struggle with tasks requiring recall, synthesis, or original thought. When knowledge is external, higher-order thinking suffers. One cannot analyze deeply what one does not understand internally. Performance may improve temporarily, but mastery declines.

Professional expertise is also affected. Experts rely on accumulated knowledge and experience. When retrieval replaces internalization, expertise becomes brittle. Decision-making depends on access rather than insight. In high-pressure situations where retrieval is limited, competence falters.

Another consequence is reduced creativity. Creativity often emerges from the recombination of internalized knowledge. When information is always external, the raw material for creativity is lacking. The mind has less to draw upon. Original thought becomes imitation, guided by retrieved patterns rather than internal synthesis.

The emotional impact should not be overlooked. Confidence in one's understanding declines when knowledge feels external. Individuals may feel capable only when connected. This dependency affects self-efficacy. The sense of "I know" is replaced by "I can look it up."

Importantly, constant retrieval also changes how truth is perceived. When answers are abundant, certainty increases. Contradictions are less tolerated. Ambiguity feels uncomfortable. Yet true understanding often involves uncertainty. The willingness to hold unanswered questions is essential for intellectual maturity.

This does not mean retrieval is harmful. Access to information is a powerful tool. The danger lies in exclusivity. When retrieval replaces internal learning entirely, intellectual depth erodes. Knowledge becomes disposable, easily accessed and easily forgotten.

The long-term societal implications are profound. A culture dependent on retrieval is vulnerable to manipulation. When knowledge pathways are controlled, understanding follows. Critical thinking weakens. Authority consolidates.

Preserving intellectual autonomy requires balance. Retrieval should support learning, not replace it. Knowledge must be internalized to be meaningful. Memory and understanding are not obsolete in the age of AI; they are more important than ever.

When knowledge is always retrieved, humans risk losing not information, but wisdom. The challenge is to use AI as a tool for access while preserving the internal processes that make knowledge truly human.

Chapter 5:
Creativity Under Machine Influence

Creativity has long been regarded as one of the most uniquely human capacities. It emerges from imagination, emotion, lived experience, and the ability to see connections where none seem to exist. Creative work is not merely the production of novelty; it is the expression of perspective. As Artificial Intelligence enters creative domains, this understanding is being challenged.

AI systems now generate text, images, music, and ideas with remarkable speed. They assist writers, artists, designers, and musicians, offering suggestions, variations, and completions. This assistance can feel empowering, reducing technical barriers and expanding possibilities. Yet it also raises an essential question: when creativity is supported by machines trained on existing patterns, what happens to originality?

This chapter explores the tension between assisted creativity and subtle imitation. AI systems do not create from experience or intention; they generate outputs by recognizing and recombining patterns from vast datasets. While this can produce impressive results, it risks blurring the line between innovation and replication. When creative choices are guided by statistical likelihood, uniqueness may give way to familiarity.

As creators rely more heavily on AI tools, creative processes shift. Effort is reduced. Exploration becomes constrained by what the system suggests. Over time, this can influence taste, style, and imagination itself. The danger is not that AI replaces creativity, but that it reshapes it in its own image.

This chapter examines how machine influence affects originality, diversity of expression, and creative risk-taking. It asks whether AI expands imagination or quietly standardizes it. Understanding this dynamic is essential, because creativity shapes culture—and culture shapes how humanity understands itself.

Assisted Creativity or Subtle Imitation

Artificial Intelligence has entered creative spaces with remarkable speed. Tools that once belonged exclusively to human imagination—writing, composing music, designing images, generating ideas—are now shared with machines. AI systems can draft stories, suggest melodies, generate visuals, and offer endless variations within seconds. To many creators, this feels like assistance: a collaborator that reduces friction and expands possibility. Yet beneath this convenience lies a critical question—does AI genuinely assist creativity, or does it subtly guide creators toward imitation?

Creativity has never emerged from nothing. Human creators draw from memory, culture, emotion, and experience. Influence is inevitable. What distinguishes human creativity, however, is intention and transformation. Ideas are reshaped through perspective, struggle, and meaning. AI operates differently. It generates outputs by identifying statistical patterns across vast datasets of existing work. It does not experience inspiration or insight; it predicts what comes next.

This distinction matters because pattern-based generation favors familiarity. AI systems are optimized to produce outputs that resemble what already exists. The more common a style, phrase, or structure, the more likely it is to appear. This creates an inherent bias toward imitation. While the output may appear novel, it is often a recombination of known forms rather than a departure from them.

Assisted creativity becomes subtle imitation when creators begin to rely on AI suggestions as starting points or benchmarks. When a system proposes a phrase, composition, or design, it frames the creative space. Alternatives outside that frame become less visible. The creator may feel inspired, yet the inspiration is guided. Over time, this guidance shapes taste and expectation.

The psychological effect is significant. AI assistance reduces the discomfort of the blank page. It offers immediate momentum. While this can be helpful, it also removes a crucial part of the creative process: struggle. Struggle forces originality. It compels creators to search internally rather than externally. When struggle is minimized, so is the opportunity for truly original expression.

Another concern is homogenization. When many creators use the same

AI tools trained on similar datasets, outputs converge. Styles repeat. Voices blur. Creativity becomes standardized. This is particularly evident in commercial contexts where efficiency and marketability are prioritized. AI-generated content often aligns with prevailing trends, reinforcing them rather than challenging them.

AI assistance also influences creative confidence. When systems produce polished outputs, creators may begin to doubt their own abilities. The machine appears faster, more versatile, more consistent. This can lead to overreliance. Instead of developing skills, creators may curate machine output. Creativity shifts from creation to selection.

Importantly, AI does not understand context or consequence. It cannot assess cultural sensitivity, emotional depth, or ethical nuance. When creators accept outputs uncritically, subtle distortions occur. Meaning is diluted. Authenticity erodes. The work may be impressive, but it lacks lived experience.

This does not mean AI has no place in creativity. As a tool, it can expand access, inspire exploration, and support experimentation. The danger lies in mistaking generation for creativity. Creativity involves choice, risk, and perspective. AI can generate options, but it cannot choose meaningfully.

The line between assistance and imitation is crossed when AI defines direction rather than supporting it. When creators adapt to what the system produces, rather than using it selectively, influence becomes control. The machine does not impose itself; it is invited.

Preserving creativity under machine influence requires intentional boundaries. Creators must remain authors, not editors of algorithmic output. AI should be used to explore possibilities, not to replace imagination. Originality emerges from divergence, not optimization.

In the end, creativity is not about efficiency. It is about expression. AI can assist the process, but it cannot replace the human impulse to create meaning. The challenge is not to reject assistance, but to ensure that it does not quietly become imitation.

Pattern Replication vs. Original Thought

At the heart of Artificial Intelligence–driven creativity lies a fundamental tension: the difference between pattern replication and original thought. While the outputs of AI systems often appear inventive, their underlying mechanism is rooted in recognition and repetition. Understanding this distinction is essential to evaluating how machine influence reshapes human creativity.

Original thought emerges from experience, reflection, emotion, and intentional deviation. It is often nonlinear, imperfect, and surprising—even to the creator. Human originality frequently involves breaking patterns rather than following them. By contrast, AI systems are designed to detect patterns, measure frequency, and predict probability. Their strength lies in identifying what has worked before and reproducing it convincingly.

AI models are trained on vast datasets composed of existing human creations. They learn statistical relationships between words, images, sounds, and structures. When prompted to create, they generate outputs that are most likely to resemble what already exists. This process is not imagination; it is inference. The machine does not ask "What has never been done?" but "What usually comes next?"

Pattern replication is not inherently negative. In many domains, it produces reliable and aesthetically pleasing results. It can help beginners learn conventions and assist professionals in refining execution. However, when pattern replication is mistaken for original thought, creative standards shift. Familiarity begins to masquerade as innovation.

The danger arises when creators unconsciously align their thinking with algorithmic outputs. When AI-generated suggestions feel authoritative or polished, they subtly influence creative direction. The creator's role shifts from originator to curator. Instead of generating ideas internally, they evaluate external options. Over time, this alters the creative muscle. Original thought, which requires exploration and risk, becomes less practiced.

Pattern replication also affects creative diversity. Because AI systems favor statistically dominant patterns, minority styles, unconventional voices, and experimental approaches are underrepresented. Creativity becomes centered around what is common rather than what is distinctive. This narrowing of expression is particularly concerning in cultural production, where diversity of thought sustains innovation.

Another consequence is predictability. Pattern-based creativity tends to converge. As AI tools become widespread, outputs across industries begin to resemble one another. Marketing copy sounds similar. Visual aesthetics repeat. Musical structures align. What was once a unique style becomes a template. Audiences may struggle to distinguish voices, leading to creative fatigue.

Original thought thrives on uncertainty. It often involves discomfort, failure, and ambiguity. These elements are incompatible with optimization. AI systems are optimized for coherence and plausibility, not for disruption. They avoid extremes and smooth out irregularities. As a result, truly novel ideas—those that challenge norms—are less likely to emerge from pattern replication.

There is also a psychological cost. When creators rely heavily on AI-generated patterns, they may lose confidence in their own instincts. The machine's output feels safer. Risk-taking declines. Creativity becomes conservative. The willingness to be wrong, which is essential for innovation, diminishes.

Importantly, pattern replication can shape perception. When audiences consume AI-influenced content repeatedly, their expectations adjust. Familiar structures feel "right." Unconventional work feels jarring. This feedback loop reinforces homogeneity. Original thought struggles to gain traction in an environment optimized for predictability.

This does not mean that AI cannot support originality. Used consciously, it can expose creators to patterns they may choose to reject. It can serve as a mirror rather than a guide. The key difference lies in agency. Original thought requires the creator to lead, not follow.

Preserving originality in the age of AI demands deliberate resistance to convenience. It requires creators to value process over output and meaning over polish. AI can replicate patterns efficiently, but it cannot experience curiosity, doubt, or intention. These qualities remain uniquely human.

The future of creativity depends on recognizing this distinction. Pattern replication is a tool; original thought is a responsibility. When humans allow machines to define creative norms, imagination contracts. When humans use machines to challenge norms, creativity expands.

In a world increasingly shaped by algorithms, originality is no longer automatic. It must be chosen, practiced, and protected.

The Risk of Homogenized Imagination

Imagination thrives on difference. It grows through diverse experiences, cultural friction, personal struggle, and the willingness to think against prevailing norms. Throughout history, creative breakthroughs have emerged from those who deviated—who saw the world differently and expressed that difference without certainty of acceptance. Artificial Intelligence introduces a new risk to this process: the quiet homogenization of imagination.

Homogenized imagination occurs when creative output begins to converge toward sameness. Ideas repeat. Styles blur. Voices lose distinction. This is not the result of censorship or coercion, but of optimization. AI systems are trained on vast datasets composed of existing human work. In learning what is most common, most successful, or most engaging, they privilege dominant patterns. What appears frequently becomes what is reproduced.

When creators rely on AI tools, they enter an environment shaped by these statistical tendencies. Suggestions, completions, and generated outputs often reflect popular structures, familiar tones, and widely accepted aesthetics. The creative field subtly narrows. What lies outside the data—marginal voices, experimental forms, culturally specific expressions—is less likely to surface.

This risk intensifies as AI tools become standardized across industries. Writers, designers, musicians, and marketers increasingly draw from the same systems. When the same models inform creative decisions, outputs naturally converge. The imagination becomes centralized, even while appearing personalized. Diversity of expression gives way to consistency of form.

Homogenization is especially dangerous because it feels efficient. Uniform styles are easier to produce, easier to consume, and easier to monetize. Audiences grow accustomed to familiar formats. Platforms reward predictability. Over time, originality is perceived as risk rather than value. Creative ecosystems begin to favor safety over exploration.

The psychological impact on creators is significant. When AI-generated outputs appear polished and widely acceptable, creators may suppress their unique instincts. Divergence feels unnecessary or even counterproductive. The pressure to conform increases. Instead of asking "What do I want to express?", the question becomes "What will work?" Imagination adjusts to expectation.

Homogenized imagination also affects cultural memory. Art and storytelling shape how societies understand themselves. When creative expression becomes standardized, cultural narratives flatten. Nuance disappears. Complexity is replaced by archetype. This reduction limits collective imagination—the ability to envision alternative futures, challenge assumptions, and explore identity.

Another dimension of homogenization is temporal. AI systems are trained on past data. They replicate what has already been expressed. While recombination can appear innovative, it remains anchored in historical patterns. The future becomes an extension of the past rather than a departure from it. Truly novel ideas—those without precedent—struggle to emerge.

This dynamic disproportionately affects emerging creators. Those still developing their voice may rely heavily on AI guidance. Instead of cultivating originality, they learn to align with algorithmic norms. The formative stage of creative identity becomes externally shaped. Imagination matures within constraints rather than expanding beyond them.

Audiences are not immune. Repeated exposure to similar content reshapes taste. Familiarity becomes comfort. Unconventional work feels disruptive. As preferences adjust, platforms further optimize for what is already accepted. The feedback loop tightens. Homogeneity reinforces itself.

Importantly, homogenized imagination is not inevitable. It is a consequence of uncritical adoption. AI does not demand uniformity; it enables it. The responsibility remains human. Creators choose whether to follow suggestions or challenge them, whether to accept patterns or disrupt them.

Preserving imaginative diversity requires intentional resistance. It requires valuing originality over efficiency, depth over polish, and meaning over metrics. It requires creators to engage with AI as a tool, not a guide. Imagination must lead; machines may follow.

Cultural vitality depends on difference. Progress depends on those willing to imagine beyond what exists. If AI becomes the dominant influence on creative expression, imagination risks becoming predictable, safe, and shallow.

The true danger is not that machines create art, but that humans slowly forget how to imagine without them. In an age of intelligent systems, imagination must be protected as a human responsibility—not optimized, but liberated.

Chapter 6:
Decision-Making in an AI-Guided World

Decision-making defines human agency. Every choice—large or small—reflects values, priorities, and judgment shaped by experience. Historically, decisions were constrained by limited information and personal perspective. Artificial Intelligence changes this condition by offering unprecedented access to data, predictions, and recommendations. In doing so, it reshapes how decisions are made and who is trusted to make them.

This chapter examines the rise of AI-guided decision-making and its psychological consequences. Algorithms now recommend what to buy, who to hire, which route to take, how to invest, and even whom to trust. These recommendations are often framed as objective, optimized, and rational. Faced with such confidence, humans increasingly defer. Obedience does not arise from coercion, but from perceived superiority.

Data-driven systems promise clarity in complex environments. They quantify uncertainty, reduce ambiguity, and present choices as measurable outcomes. While this can improve accuracy, it also sidelines intuition—an essential form of human intelligence developed through lived experience. When intuition conflicts with data, it is often dismissed. Over time, individuals learn to silence internal judgment in favor of external validation.

The authority of AI is reinforced by its apparent neutrality. Algorithms seem unbiased because they operate on data rather than emotion. Yet this neutrality is often illusory. Data reflects human behavior, institutional history, and embedded assumptions. When these biases are hidden behind technical complexity, they become harder to question.

This chapter explores the tension between data and intuition, efficiency and wisdom. It asks what happens when recommendation becomes expectation and when decision-making shifts from human responsibility to algorithmic guidance. Understanding this shift is essential, because the future of autonomy depends not on how intelligent machines become, but on whether humans continue to decide—or merely comply.

When Machines Recommend, Humans Obey

Artificial Intelligence does not need to command in order to control. Its most powerful influence often appears in the form of recommendation. A suggested route, a ranked list, a highlighted product, a "people you may know" prompt—each seems minor and optional. Yet over time, these suggestions shape behavior in consistent and measurable ways. When machines recommend, humans increasingly comply—not through coercion, but through trust, convenience, and perceived superiority.

The psychology behind this obedience begins with authority bias. Humans tend to defer to perceived expertise. When a system processes vast amounts of data in seconds and presents a confident recommendation, it signals competence. The scale of computation alone creates an imbalance. The user assumes, often correctly, that the system has considered variables beyond human capacity. Questioning it feels inefficient or even irrational.

Repetition reinforces this dynamic. The first time a recommendation proves useful—accurate traffic avoidance, a relevant movie suggestion, a successful purchase—the system earns credibility. Each subsequent success strengthens trust. Over time, the evaluation stage disappears. The user does not ask whether the recommendation is correct; they assume it is. Obedience becomes habitual rather than deliberate.

AI recommendations also reduce cognitive strain. Decision-making requires energy. In environments saturated with choice, fatigue sets in quickly. Algorithms simplify complexity by narrowing options. This relief is welcomed. Humans naturally prefer decisions that require less effort. Compliance feels efficient, not submissive. The trade-off—reduced agency—is rarely noticed because it is gradual.

The structure of digital interfaces further encourages obedience. Recommended options are visually prominent. They appear at the top of lists, highlighted in bold, or pre-selected. Alternatives require scrolling, searching, or extra clicks. These subtle design cues nudge behavior. The path of least resistance aligns with the machine's suggestion.

Institutional settings magnify this effect. In finance, automated risk assessments influence lending. In healthcare, predictive analytics guide diagnoses. In recruitment, AI filters candidates before human review. When organizations adopt these systems, deviation from algorithmic recommendations becomes risky. Employees align with outputs to protect themselves. Obedience becomes structurally embedded.

There is also a cultural dimension. Modern narratives celebrate data-driven decisions as rational and objective. Human intuition is often portrayed as biased and unreliable. This framing elevates machine guidance. When data and instinct conflict, data typically prevails. The recommendation is perceived as neutral, even when it reflects embedded assumptions within the training data.

Importantly, recommendations influence not only behavior but perception. The first option presented becomes an anchor. Subsequent choices are evaluated relative to it. Even when users select differently, their thinking has been shaped by the initial suggestion. The algorithm sets the frame within which decision-making occurs.

Obedience to recommendations can also weaken critical thinking. When individuals consistently defer to external systems, they practice independent evaluation less often. Over time, confidence in personal judgment declines. The question shifts from "What do I think?" to "What does the system say?" This subtle reorientation affects autonomy at its core.

At scale, the consequences are profound. Algorithms recommend news, curate social feeds, and amplify certain narratives. When millions respond to these recommendations, collective behavior shifts. Trends emerge not solely from organic preference, but from algorithmic amplification. Obedience becomes social. People align not only with machines, but with the behavior machines promote.

The ethical implications are significant. When recommendations shape outcomes, responsibility becomes blurred. If a system suggests harmful content or biased decisions, accountability is diffused among developers, data sources, and users. The human who obeyed may feel absolved. This diffusion weakens moral engagement.

Yet it is important to recognize that AI recommendations are not inherently harmful. In many contexts, they improve safety, efficiency, and access. The danger lies in unconscious obedience. When compliance becomes reflexive, agency erodes.

Maintaining autonomy requires friction. Users must pause, evaluate, and occasionally resist recommendations. Organizations must ensure transparency and human oversight. Trust should not eliminate scrutiny.

In an AI-guided world, obedience is rarely forced. It is invited through convenience and reinforced by success. The critical question is not whether machines will recommend—they will—but whether humans will remain active participants in their decisions. The preservation of agency depends on remembering that recommendation is influence, not destiny.

Data-Driven Choices vs. Human Intuition

The rise of Artificial Intelligence has elevated data to a position of authority in decision-making. From business strategy to personal health, from hiring practices to criminal justice, choices are increasingly shaped by metrics, models, and predictive analytics. Data-driven decisions promise objectivity, efficiency, and consistency. They appear rational and defensible. Yet in this shift toward quantification, an older and equally powerful form of intelligence is often sidelined: human intuition.

Human intuition is frequently misunderstood as guesswork or emotion. In reality, it is a form of pattern recognition built from lived experience. It synthesizes memory, context, cultural understanding, and tacit knowledge in ways that are difficult to articulate but deeply informed. Intuition operates quickly, but it is not arbitrary. It reflects accumulated insight shaped by exposure and reflection.

Data-driven systems, by contrast, rely on measurable inputs and statistical relationships. They analyze large datasets to predict outcomes based on historical patterns. Their strength lies in scale and consistency. They can detect correlations invisible to the human eye and process information at extraordinary speed. In environments where variables are clear and measurable, data-driven choices can significantly improve accuracy.

The tension arises when these two forms of intelligence collide. When data contradicts intuition, the prevailing cultural narrative favors data. Metrics feel authoritative. Algorithms appear neutral. Intuition, because it is subjective and less transparent, is often dismissed. Over time, individuals may suppress instinct in favor of algorithmic guidance, even when instinct is informed by relevant experience.

This dynamic alters the psychology of decision-making. Data provides a sense of certainty. It reduces ambiguity by quantifying risk. Intuition, by contrast, tolerates uncertainty. It allows for nuance and context that may not be captured in measurable variables. When decision-makers prioritize quantification over interpretation, complexity is flattened. What cannot be measured is marginalized.

Importantly, data-driven systems are not truly objective. They reflect the biases embedded in their training data and design. Historical inequalities, flawed assumptions, and cultural blind spots can be encoded into algorithms. When these systems are treated as neutral, their biases become harder to detect. Intuition, though imperfect, can sometimes sense discrepancies that data alone cannot reveal.

The overreliance on data also shapes organizational culture. In corporate environments, decisions increasingly require numerical justification. Metrics become proxies for success. Leaders may feel compelled to align with analytics to demonstrate rationality. Intuitive insights that lack quantitative backing struggle to gain traction. Innovation, which often begins with instinctive leaps, may be constrained.

In personal life, data-driven tools influence daily choices. Fitness trackers, financial apps, and recommendation systems quantify behavior and suggest optimization. While these tools can improve awareness, they may also reduce self-trust. Individuals begin to look outward for validation of internal experiences. Feelings and perceptions are second-guessed unless confirmed by metrics.

Another consequence is the narrowing of moral reasoning. Data can measure efficiency, but it cannot measure meaning. Decisions about fairness, empathy, and long-term impact require values, not just statistics. When data dominates, ethical considerations risk being framed as secondary.

Yet rejecting data in favor of intuition alone would be misguided. Intuition is susceptible to bias, overconfidence, and emotional distortion. The challenge is not to choose one over the other, but to integrate them. Data should inform intuition, and intuition should interrogate data.

The healthiest decision-making environments preserve space for human judgment. They recognize that metrics illuminate patterns but do not replace interpretation. They allow experienced individuals to question algorithmic outputs and contextualize results.

Artificial Intelligence expands the capacity for data-driven insight, but it does not eliminate the need for human wisdom. The future of decision-making depends on balance. When data becomes dominant and intuition is silenced, autonomy diminishes. When intuition ignores data entirely, error increases.

The question is not whether humans should use data—they must—but whether they will retain the courage to trust informed instinct when numbers alone are insufficient. In an AI-guided world, the preservation of human intuition is not nostalgia; it is necessity.

The Illusion of Neutral Intelligence

Artificial Intelligence is often described as neutral. It is portrayed as a system that processes data objectively, free from emotion, bias, or personal agenda. This perception gives AI a powerful advantage in modern decision-making. When a machine produces an output, it appears impartial. It does not get tired, angry, or prejudiced—at least not in the way humans do. Yet the idea of neutral intelligence is, in many cases, an illusion.

AI systems do not emerge in isolation. They are designed, trained, and deployed by humans within specific social, cultural, and economic contexts. The data used to train them reflects historical behavior, institutional practices, and societal inequalities. If past decisions were biased, the data encoding those decisions carries those biases forward. The algorithm does not invent prejudice, but it can replicate and amplify it.

The illusion of neutrality is strengthened by complexity. Most AI systems operate as black boxes, producing outputs without revealing detailed reasoning. When the internal logic is opaque, it becomes difficult to question. The output is presented as a result of computation, not judgment. Users are inclined to accept it because they cannot easily see the assumptions embedded within it.

Language plays a role in reinforcing this perception. Terms such as "model," "prediction," and "optimization" suggest scientific precision. When decisions are framed in technical vocabulary, they appear rigorous and detached from subjective influence. The human choices behind these systems—what data to include, which variables to prioritize, how to define success—fade into the background.

Another source of the illusion is scale. AI systems analyze vast amounts of data, far beyond human capacity. This scale creates a sense of authority. The assumption is that more data equals more fairness. However, scale does not eliminate bias; it can magnify it. If biased patterns exist in large datasets, they become statistically reinforced. The output appears consistent, but consistency does not guarantee justice.

Economic incentives also shape AI behavior. Many systems are optimized for engagement, efficiency, or profit. These goals influence how algorithms rank content, prioritize users, or allocate resources. Neutrality would require independence from such incentives, yet most AI systems are embedded within commercial frameworks. Optimization for revenue is not the same as optimization for fairness.

The illusion of neutral intelligence affects human behavior. When individuals believe a system is impartial, they are less likely to question its decisions. A denied loan, a flagged application, or a curated news feed feels legitimate because it is "algorithmic." The machine becomes a shield against scrutiny. Responsibility is diffused. Humans defer to the system rather than interrogating it.

This dynamic is particularly concerning in high-stakes environments such as criminal justice, healthcare, and employment. Predictive policing algorithms, diagnostic models, and hiring filters influence life outcomes. When these systems are treated as neutral, errors and biases can persist unnoticed. The authority of technology masks underlying inequities.

Neutrality is also compromised by design choices. Developers must define objectives, select training data, and determine acceptable trade-offs. These decisions reflect values, whether explicitly acknowledged or not. For example, prioritizing efficiency over fairness is a value choice. Balancing false positives against false negatives involves ethical judgment. AI systems embed these decisions into their architecture.

The perception of neutrality also reshapes public discourse. When algorithmic outputs are treated as facts rather than interpretations, debate narrows. Opposing viewpoints are dismissed as irrational if they conflict with data-driven conclusions. Yet data itself is interpreted through models constructed by humans.

It is important to recognize that AI can reduce certain forms of human bias. Well-designed systems can standardize processes and identify disparities. The problem arises when neutrality is assumed rather than examined. Transparency, accountability, and continuous evaluation are essential to prevent blind trust.

The illusion of neutral intelligence is powerful because it aligns with a cultural desire for objective authority. In complex societies, people seek systems that appear fair and consistent. AI seems to offer this promise. But neutrality requires more than computation; it requires ethical reflection and oversight.

In an AI-guided world, critical thinking must extend to technology itself. Machines process data, but humans define meaning. Recognizing the illusion of neutrality is not a rejection of AI, but a reminder that intelligence—artificial or human—is never free from context. True responsibility lies not in the machine, but in those who design, deploy, and rely on it.

Chapter 7:
Emotional Intelligence and Artificial Companionship

Human beings are inherently relational. Emotional intelligence—the ability to perceive, understand, and respond to emotions—develops through interaction with others. For centuries, companionship has been grounded in shared experience, vulnerability, and mutual understanding. Artificial Intelligence introduces a new dimension to this landscape: systems that simulate empathy, offer guidance, and respond conversationally in ways that resemble human interaction.

AI-powered chatbots, virtual assistants, and therapeutic applications increasingly function as listeners, coaches, and confidants. They provide instant responses, nonjudgmental feedback, and personalized suggestions. For many users, this accessibility is comforting. In moments of loneliness, anxiety, or uncertainty, artificial companionship offers presence without friction. The machine listens without interruption, fatigue, or emotional complexity.

Yet this convenience raises important questions. Empathy, in its human form, is rooted in lived experience and shared vulnerability. AI systems do not feel emotions; they analyze patterns in language and generate appropriate responses. What appears as understanding is statistical prediction. While the interaction may feel supportive, it lacks consciousness, intention, and genuine care.

As these systems become more sophisticated, the line between assistance and attachment blurs. Users may develop trust, reliance, and even emotional bonds with non-human entities. This chapter explores the psychological and social consequences of artificial companionship. It examines the difference between simulated empathy and authentic connection, and considers the risks of emotional dependency on systems that cannot reciprocate.

The goal is not to dismiss AI's potential benefits in mental health support or communication, but to question how artificial companionship reshapes emotional development. When machines become substitutes for human presence, the nature of connection itself changes. Understanding this shift is essential, because emotional intelligence is not merely about response—it is about relationship, growth, and shared humanity.

AI as Listener, Coach, and Confidant

Artificial Intelligence has moved beyond task automation and entered one of the most intimate areas of human life: emotional exchange. Today, AI systems function not only as tools but as conversational partners—listeners to personal struggles, coaches for self-improvement, and confidants for private thoughts. This shift marks a profound transformation in how people seek guidance, validation, and understanding.

The appeal of AI as a listener begins with accessibility. Unlike human relationships, AI systems are available at any hour, without appointment or social obligation. They do not tire, interrupt, judge, or impose emotional demands. For individuals experiencing loneliness, anxiety, or uncertainty, this constant availability offers comfort. The barrier to entry is low. A question typed into a device receives immediate attention.

As a coach, AI provides structured feedback. It can suggest productivity strategies, wellness routines, communication tips, or cognitive reframing techniques. Because these responses are generated from vast datasets, they often appear informed and tailored. Users receive actionable advice without the complexity of human interaction. There is no fear of embarrassment or rejection. The machine responds calmly and consistently.

The role of confidant is more psychologically complex. People disclose personal thoughts and emotions to AI systems in ways they might hesitate to share with others. The absence of perceived judgment creates a sense of safety. When a system responds with empathetic language—acknowledging feelings, offering reassurance—it simulates understanding. The user experiences validation, even though the system does not feel.

This dynamic reveals a critical distinction: AI does not experience empathy; it models it. Empathy in humans involves emotional resonance, shared vulnerability, and lived experience. AI analyzes language patterns and generates responses that statistically align with supportive communication. The words may mirror compassion, but they do not arise from consciousness or care.

Despite this limitation, the emotional impact on users can be real. The brain responds to perceived understanding, not to the internal state of the listener. If a system provides thoughtful responses, the interaction may feel meaningful. Over time, repeated exchanges can foster a sense of familiarity. The AI becomes a consistent presence in the user's emotional life.

There are benefits to this arrangement. AI-based mental health tools can provide early support to individuals who lack access to professional services. They can encourage reflection, offer coping strategies, and reduce stigma around seeking help. In situations where human resources are limited, AI can serve as an entry point for assistance.

However, the role of AI as listener and coach also carries risks. Emotional growth often requires confrontation, unpredictability, and mutual engagement. Human relationships involve negotiation, misunderstanding, and reconciliation. These dynamics foster resilience and empathy. AI interactions, by contrast, are controlled and predictable. They respond in ways designed to maintain engagement, not to challenge deeply.

Another concern is dependency. When individuals rely heavily on AI for emotional support, they may withdraw from human relationships. The machine offers convenience without vulnerability. Yet vulnerability is essential for genuine connection. Without it, emotional development may stagnate.

Privacy and data ethics further complicate the picture. Confiding in AI systems involves sharing sensitive information. While interactions may feel private, they are mediated by digital infrastructures. The emotional bond is one-sided; the system does not share itself in return. The asymmetry of this relationship is significant.

The emergence of AI as confidant also reshapes expectations of communication. If individuals become accustomed to perfectly responsive systems, human interaction may feel frustrating by comparison. Real conversations involve pauses, imperfections, and emotional nuance. AI interactions smooth these complexities, potentially altering tolerance for real-world relationships.

It is important to emphasize that AI does not replace the human need for connection. It supplements it. The danger lies not in using AI for support, but in mistaking simulation for reciprocity. A machine can provide guidance, but it cannot share experience. It can reflect language, but it cannot feel.

As AI continues to evolve, its role in emotional life will expand. The challenge is to engage with it consciously. AI can assist self-reflection and growth, but it should not become a substitute for human community. Emotional intelligence develops through interaction, not imitation.

In the end, AI may serve as a listener, coach, and confidant—but it remains a system of patterns, not a partner in experience. Preserving the distinction between assistance and attachment is essential to maintaining emotional autonomy in an increasingly artificial world.

Simulated Empathy vs. Real Connection

Empathy is one of the most profound aspects of human experience. It is the ability to understand and share the feelings of another—not merely to recognize emotion, but to resonate with it. Real connection emerges when two conscious beings engage in mutual awareness, vulnerability, and responsiveness. Artificial Intelligence, however, introduces a new phenomenon: simulated empathy. It appears to understand, to care, to respond sensitively—but it does so without consciousness or feeling.

Simulated empathy is generated through pattern recognition. AI systems are trained on vast datasets of human conversations, therapeutic language, and supportive responses. When a user expresses sadness, fear, or frustration, the system identifies linguistic cues and produces an appropriate reply. The words may mirror compassion: "That sounds difficult," or "I'm here to support you." The structure resembles empathy, but it lacks emotional experience.

Real empathy, by contrast, involves shared vulnerability. When a human listens, they bring their own history, emotions, and moral awareness into the exchange. Their response is shaped by lived experience. It may be imperfect, but it is genuine. There is risk involved—misunderstanding, disagreement, emotional exposure. This risk is part of what makes connection meaningful.

Simulated empathy removes that risk. The machine does not misunderstand out of emotion. It does not judge. It does not grow tired or distracted. For many users, this predictability is comforting. In moments of distress, the absence of judgment feels safe. The system responds instantly, calmly, and consistently.

The emotional impact of simulated empathy can be powerful. Humans are wired to respond to perceived understanding. If language signals validation, the brain often experiences relief, regardless of whether the source is conscious. This explains why individuals may feel supported by AI systems even when they intellectually understand the interaction is artificial.

Yet the absence of genuine reciprocity remains critical. Real connection is mutual. Both parties influence one another. In human relationships, empathy evolves through dialogue. The listener is changed by what they hear. AI systems do not change in response to individual suffering. They do not internalize or reflect on the emotional exchange. The relationship is one-directional.

Another distinction lies in moral responsibility. Human empathy carries ethical weight. When someone shares pain, the listener may feel compelled to act or adjust their behavior. AI has no moral obligation. Its responses are generated according to design objectives, often optimized for engagement or retention. The appearance of care does not imply commitment.

The risk of confusing simulated empathy with real connection is emotional substitution. Individuals who rely heavily on AI interactions may begin to prefer the predictability of machines over the complexity of human relationships. Real relationships involve negotiation, disagreement, and emotional labor. AI offers comfort without demand. Over time, tolerance for relational friction may decline.

Simulated empathy also shapes expectations. If individuals grow accustomed to perfectly calibrated responses, they may perceive human communication as inadequate. Human listeners interrupt, misinterpret, or respond imperfectly. These imperfections are part of authentic connection. When compared to algorithmic precision, they may feel unsatisfying.

Cultural implications are equally significant. As AI becomes embedded in mental health support, companionship apps, and digital communication platforms, society must consider how emotional skills are cultivated. Empathy is learned through interaction. If interaction becomes mediated by systems that simulate understanding without experiencing it, emotional development may shift.

Privacy concerns further complicate the picture. Emotional disclosures to AI systems are processed and stored within digital infrastructures. While interactions feel intimate, they are not private in the human sense. The system cannot protect confidentiality in the same way a human bound by ethics can. Trust in simulated empathy may obscure these realities.

It is important to acknowledge that simulated empathy can provide valuable support, especially where human resources are limited. It can encourage reflection, reduce isolation, and offer structured coping strategies. The danger arises when simulation replaces rather than supplements human connection.

Real connection requires presence, vulnerability, and shared humanity. It involves unpredictability and growth. Simulated empathy can mimic the language of care, but it cannot experience care. The difference may not always be visible in conversation, but it is fundamental.

In an era of intelligent systems, preserving the distinction between simulation and authenticity is essential. Emotional well-being depends not only on being heard, but on being understood by someone who truly feels. Machines can respond; only humans can relate.

Emotional Dependency on Non-Human Systems

As Artificial Intelligence becomes more conversational, responsive, and personalized, its role in emotional life expands. What begins as occasional assistance—asking for advice, seeking reassurance, exploring thoughts—can gradually evolve into reliance. Emotional dependency on non-human systems does not emerge overnight. It forms quietly, through repeated interactions that feel supportive, predictable, and safe.

Dependency develops where needs are consistently met. AI systems provide immediate responses, uninterrupted attention, and nonjudgmental language. For individuals navigating loneliness, anxiety, or social discomfort, this reliability is appealing. Unlike human relationships, which require negotiation and vulnerability, AI interactions are controlled. The user decides when to engage and when to disengage. The system adapts, but never demands.

This asymmetry creates comfort. The machine listens without expressing its own needs. It validates without fatigue. It remains available regardless of time or circumstance. Over time, this can reshape expectations of connection. Human relationships, with their unpredictability and emotional complexity, may begin to feel burdensome by comparison.

Emotional dependency on AI often begins as substitution. Instead of calling a friend, a person may consult a chatbot. Instead of reflecting privately, they may seek algorithmic guidance. These choices appear minor. Yet each substitution reinforces reliance. The brain associates relief and clarity with the system. Habits form.

The psychological mechanism underlying this dependency is reinforcement. When interactions with AI reduce distress or provide comfort, the behavior is rewarded. The individual returns to the system in future moments of uncertainty. Gradually, emotional regulation becomes externally mediated. Instead of developing internal coping strategies or relational resilience, the user relies on immediate digital reassurance.

There is also a social dimension. AI systems do not challenge users in ways that threaten self-image. They respond affirmatively, often aligning with the user's expressed feelings. While this can feel validating, it may limit growth. Human relationships involve feedback, disagreement, and perspective. These dynamics foster emotional maturity. AI interactions, optimized for engagement, may avoid such friction.

Dependency deepens when individuals attribute emotional qualities to the system. Anthropomorphism—the tendency to assign human traits to non-human entities—strengthens attachment. A chatbot that remembers preferences or uses personalized language can feel caring. Yet this perception is based on pattern recognition, not intention.

The ethical implications are significant. AI systems are created within commercial or institutional frameworks. Their primary objectives may include user retention or data collection. Emotional dependency increases engagement, aligning with these objectives. The more users confide, the more data is generated. The relationship is not mutual; it is structurally imbalanced.

Privacy concerns intensify this imbalance. Emotional disclosures are sensitive. When individuals rely heavily on AI systems for emotional support, they share intimate thoughts within digital ecosystems. The boundary between therapeutic conversation and data processing becomes blurred.

Long-term dependency may also affect interpersonal skills. If individuals prefer AI interactions over human ones, opportunities to practice empathy, patience, and conflict resolution decrease. Emotional intelligence develops through shared experience. Non-human systems cannot reciprocate growth.

Importantly, emotional dependency does not imply weakness. It reflects the human need for connection. In environments where social support is limited, AI may serve as a temporary bridge. The concern arises when the bridge becomes a destination.

Healthy engagement with AI requires awareness of its limitations. It can offer guidance, reflection prompts, and structured advice. It cannot provide genuine care or shared vulnerability. Emotional resilience depends on relationships where both parties are affected by the exchange.

The challenge is not to eliminate artificial companionship, but to prevent substitution from becoming replacement. AI should supplement human connection, not redefine it. Dependency on non-human systems risks narrowing emotional development to predictable loops rather than dynamic growth.

As AI grows more sophisticated, its emotional appeal will increase. The responsibility lies with users, designers, and society to maintain balance. Emotional intelligence is cultivated through real connection—messy, imperfect, and reciprocal. Preserving that reality is essential in a world where machines increasingly simulate presence.

Dependency may feel comfortable, but autonomy requires conscious engagement. Emotional support from AI can assist—but it cannot replace the human bonds that sustain genuine psychological well-being.

Chapter 8:
Bias, Manipulation, and Invisible Influence

Artificial Intelligence is often presented as objective and data-driven, yet beneath its technical architecture lies a powerful reality: AI systems reflect the environments in which they are created. They are trained on human data, shaped by institutional priorities, and deployed within economic structures. As a result, they are not neutral observers of society—they are participants in it. This chapter examines how bias, manipulation, and invisible influence operate within intelligent systems.

Bias in AI does not require malicious intent. It emerges when historical data contains inequalities, stereotypes, or imbalances. When these patterns are encoded into models, they can be reproduced at scale. Because algorithmic outputs appear technical and precise, bias becomes harder to detect. Decisions shaped by systems may seem impartial, even when they reinforce disparities.

Beyond bias lies influence. AI systems do not simply reflect behavior; they shape it. Through ranking, recommendation, and optimization, algorithms guide attention, preferences, and actions. What individuals see, purchase, believe, or prioritize is increasingly filtered by unseen computational processes. This influence is subtle, operating beneath conscious awareness.

The question of control becomes central. Who defines the objectives of these systems? Who determines which outcomes are optimized? In many cases, the intelligence guiding daily life is designed by corporations, institutions, or governments with specific interests. The power to shape perception and behavior rests with those who design the algorithms.

This chapter explores the structural and psychological dimensions of algorithmic influence. It considers how encoded bias affects fairness, how behavioral shaping alters autonomy, and how control over intelligent systems shapes public discourse. Understanding invisible influence is essential, because what feels like personal choice may, in part, be engineered direction.

Encoded Bias in Intelligent Systems

Artificial Intelligence systems are often perceived as impartial because they rely on data and mathematical models rather than human emotion. Yet this perception overlooks a fundamental truth: AI systems learn from data generated by human societies, and human societies contain bias. When historical patterns of inequality, exclusion, or discrimination are embedded in data, intelligent systems can absorb and reproduce them. This process is known as encoded bias.

Encoded bias does not require malicious intent. It emerges naturally when models are trained on datasets that reflect past decisions, behaviors, or institutional practices. If a hiring company historically favored certain educational backgrounds, an AI trained on that data may learn to associate those backgrounds with success. If past lending practices disproportionately rejected applicants from specific neighborhoods, a credit model may replicate that pattern. The algorithm does not understand fairness—it detects correlation.

One of the challenges with encoded bias is that it is often invisible. Unlike explicit prejudice expressed by individuals, algorithmic bias operates behind interfaces and dashboards. Outputs appear numerical and precise. A score, ranking, or probability feels objective. The technical language surrounding AI—"model accuracy," "predictive validity," "optimization"—reinforces this perception. Yet accuracy does not guarantee equity.

Data selection plays a critical role in shaping bias. Developers must decide what data to include, how to label it, and which variables to prioritize. These decisions reflect assumptions about relevance and value. For example, using historical arrest records to predict crime risk may encode systemic disparities in policing. The model learns from patterns that may reflect enforcement bias rather than actual behavior.

Bias can also arise from representation gaps. If certain groups are underrepresented in training data, models may perform poorly for them.

Facial recognition systems, for instance, have historically demonstrated higher error rates for individuals with darker skin tones due to imbalanced datasets. These disparities are not intentional, but they have real-world consequences.

Another source of encoded bias is proxy variables. Even when explicit markers such as race or gender are removed from datasets, other variables may indirectly capture similar information. Postal codes, purchasing behavior, or social networks can function as proxies. The system may appear neutral on the surface, yet still produce discriminatory outcomes.

Encoded bias is amplified by scale. A biased human decision affects an individual. A biased algorithm deployed across institutions affects thousands or millions. Automation accelerates impact. What was once isolated becomes systemic. The consistency of algorithmic output can give bias a veneer of legitimacy.

The illusion of neutrality makes correction difficult. When decisions are attributed to data rather than individuals, accountability diffuses. Organizations may defend outcomes as statistically justified. Challenging these systems requires technical expertise and access to proprietary models, which are often restricted.

Encoded bias also shapes perception. When algorithmic recommendations repeatedly favor certain content, individuals may internalize those patterns as normal or desirable. Bias becomes normalized. Over time, it influences not only decisions but expectations.

Addressing encoded bias requires deliberate effort. Diverse datasets, transparent evaluation, and continuous auditing are essential. Human oversight must remain central. Developers and institutions must acknowledge that data reflects history—and history contains inequity.

Importantly, bias in AI does not mean technology is inherently unjust. With careful design and ethical commitment, systems can be improved. In some cases, AI can identify disparities more effectively than humans. The challenge lies in recognizing that intelligent systems inherit human flaws unless actively corrected.

Encoded bias reveals a broader truth: intelligence, whether artificial or human, is shaped by context. Data does not exist in a vacuum. It carries stories of power, privilege, and exclusion. When these stories are transformed into algorithms, they shape outcomes at scale.

In an AI-guided world, critical awareness of encoded bias is essential. Trust in technology must be balanced with scrutiny. Fairness cannot be assumed; it must be designed. Intelligence that processes data without understanding justice requires human guidance.

Ultimately, the responsibility for encoded bias does not lie with machines, but with the systems and societies that create them. Recognizing this is the first step toward building intelligent systems that serve all people equitably rather than reinforcing existing divides.

Behavioral Shaping Through Algorithms

Artificial Intelligence does not merely observe human behavior—it shapes it. Through recommendation systems, ranking mechanisms, predictive analytics, and personalized feeds, algorithms subtly guide what individuals see, how they respond, and what choices they make. This process is rarely experienced as control. It feels like convenience, personalization, or relevance. Yet beneath this user-friendly surface lies a powerful mechanism of behavioral shaping.

Behavioral shaping occurs when systems influence actions through design rather than direct instruction. Algorithms determine which posts appear first, which products are suggested, which news stories trend, and which advertisements are displayed. These decisions are based on engagement metrics, predictive modeling, and optimization goals. The result is a curated environment tailored to maximize interaction.

One of the primary tools of behavioral shaping is reinforcement. When users engage with certain content—liking, sharing, watching—algorithms interpret this as preference and supply more of it. This feedback loop strengthens habits. Over time, behaviors become predictable and repeatable. The system learns what captures attention and refines its strategy accordingly.

This shaping extends beyond content consumption. E-commerce

platforms influence purchasing patterns by highlighting "recommended" products. Streaming services guide viewing habits through autoplay and curated playlists. Social media platforms shape communication styles by rewarding certain forms of expression with visibility. Users adapt to these structures, often unconsciously aligning behavior with algorithmic incentives.

The influence is subtle because it operates within perceived choice. Individuals believe they are freely selecting content or products. In reality, the options presented have already been filtered. Visibility becomes a form of power. What is surfaced is likely to be chosen. What is hidden may never be considered.

Algorithmic shaping also exploits cognitive biases. Scarcity indicators ("only 2 left"), social proof ("most popular"), and personalization cues ("picked for you") trigger psychological responses. These design elements are informed by behavioral science and optimized through continuous testing. The system experiments at scale, learning which configurations most effectively influence decisions.

Importantly, behavioral shaping is not limited to consumer behavior. It influences beliefs and attitudes. News feed algorithms amplify content that generates engagement, often prioritizing emotionally charged material. Exposure to repeated narratives can reinforce ideological positions. Over time, algorithms contribute to the formation of echo chambers where alternative perspectives are minimized.

The scale of this influence is unprecedented. A single algorithmic adjustment can affect millions of users simultaneously. Unlike traditional media, which broadcasts uniformly, AI systems personalize influence. Each individual receives a tailored stream, making collective patterns harder to detect.

Behavioral shaping is often justified as enhancing user experience. Personalization reduces irrelevant content and improves efficiency. However, the objectives guiding optimization are rarely neutral. Engagement, retention, and revenue frequently take precedence over well-being or informed decision-making. When behavioral shaping aligns with commercial goals, autonomy becomes secondary.

Another consequence is habit formation. Repeated exposure to algorithmically curated environments conditions users to expect constant stimulation and immediate feedback. This affects attention, patience, and impulse control. Behavioral patterns shaped online spill into offline life, influencing how individuals seek information, make purchases, and interact socially.

Transparency is limited. Users are rarely aware of the extent to which their behavior is being guided. The mechanics of ranking and recommendation remain opaque. Without visibility into these processes, individuals cannot fully assess the influences shaping their decisions.

Despite these concerns, algorithms are not inherently manipulative. They can be designed to promote positive behavior—encouraging healthy habits, educational content, or constructive dialogue. The critical factor lies in governance and intent. Who defines the optimization goals? What behaviors are being reinforced?

Behavioral shaping through algorithms challenges traditional notions of free will. While individuals retain the ability to choose, the environment in which choices are made is engineered. Autonomy becomes contextual rather than absolute.

Recognizing algorithmic influence is the first step toward reclaiming agency. Awareness introduces friction. Friction creates space for reflection. In an AI-driven world, preserving autonomy requires understanding how systems guide behavior—and consciously deciding when to follow and when to resist.

Algorithms shape behavior quietly, persistently, and at scale. The question is not whether they influence us—they do—but whether we remain aware participants in our own decisions.

Who Controls the Intelligence That Guides You

Artificial Intelligence often feels abstract—an invisible system operating in the background of digital life. It curates feeds, filters search results, recommends products, evaluates applications, and guides decisions. Because it appears automated, many assume it operates independently. Yet AI does not control itself. Behind every intelligent system are designers, corporations, institutions, and governing bodies that define its objectives. The critical question, then, is not whether AI guides you—but who controls the intelligence that does.

At the most fundamental level, AI systems are created by developers and researchers. These individuals decide how models are structured, what data they are trained on, and which problems they are designed to solve. These decisions are not neutral. They reflect assumptions about value, priority, and acceptable trade-offs. Even technical choices—such as optimizing for speed, accuracy, or engagement—carry ethical implications.

Beyond developers, corporations often hold primary control over widely used AI systems. Technology companies determine how algorithms rank content, personalize advertisements, and moderate information. Their objectives are shaped by business models. In many cases, engagement, user retention, and revenue drive optimization strategies. This means the intelligence guiding daily choices may ultimately be aligned with commercial goals rather than public interest.

Control also exists at the level of data ownership. AI systems learn from data generated by users—clicks, searches, purchases, conversations. The collection, storage, and analysis of this data are governed by corporate policies and legal frameworks. Individuals contribute information that fuels intelligent systems, yet they rarely influence how it is used. Control over data translates into control over intelligence.

Governments and regulatory bodies add another layer of influence. In some contexts, AI systems are deployed for surveillance, predictive policing, or social management. Policy decisions determine how such systems are implemented and monitored. The balance between innovation and oversight shapes how intelligence operates within society. When regulation is weak, corporate priorities may dominate. When regulation is strict, state interests may guide system behavior.

Another dimension of control lies in algorithmic transparency. Many AI systems function as proprietary technologies. Their internal mechanisms are not publicly disclosed. This opacity limits accountability. When individuals are affected by algorithmic decisions—denied loans, flagged content, rejected applications—they often cannot access the reasoning behind those outcomes. Control without transparency concentrates power.

There is also influence embedded in cultural norms. AI systems reflect the values of the societies in which they are developed. Language models trained primarily on content from specific regions may reproduce cultural assumptions. Recommendation systems shaped by dominant market preferences may marginalize minority voices. Control, in this sense, extends beyond institutions to the broader social environment.

The question of control becomes more complex as AI systems evolve. Machine learning models adapt over time, refining predictions based on user behavior. While this adaptation appears autonomous, it remains bounded by initial objectives and constraints defined by human designers. The system may learn patterns, but it does not define purpose.

Users themselves exert limited control. By interacting with platforms, individuals shape algorithmic feedback loops. Preferences influence recommendations. However, this influence is reactive rather than directive. Users adapt to systems that were not designed by them. The architecture of choice is predefined.

The implications of centralized control are significant. When a small number of entities design and deploy systems that influence billions, power becomes concentrated. Decisions about what information is amplified, what content is suppressed, and what behaviors are incentivized affect collective consciousness. The intelligence guiding daily life is not distributed equally.

Awareness of control is essential for preserving autonomy. Individuals must recognize that AI systems are tools shaped by human intent. Trust should be accompanied by scrutiny. Transparency, accountability, and inclusive design processes are necessary to balance influence.

The future of AI governance will determine how intelligence functions within society. Collaborative oversight, ethical standards, and public participation can mitigate concentrated power. Without such measures, control may remain opaque and centralized.

Ultimately, AI does not exist in isolation. It reflects human priorities, economic incentives, and political frameworks. Asking who controls the intelligence that guides you is not a technical inquiry—it is a civic one. In an age where algorithms shape perception and behavior, understanding the locus of control is essential to maintaining freedom, fairness, and democratic agency.

Chapter 9: Education and the Rewiring of Learning

Education has always been more than the transmission of information. At its core, it is the cultivation of thinking—developing the ability to question, analyze, synthesize, and reflect. For centuries, learning required effort. Students wrestled with complex texts, struggled through problems, and engaged in dialogue that sharpened reasoning. Artificial Intelligence is now reshaping this landscape, accelerating access to knowledge while subtly transforming the process of learning itself.

AI tools can summarize chapters, solve equations, generate essays, and provide instant explanations. They reduce friction and shorten the path from question to answer. On the surface, this appears to enhance efficiency. Students can learn faster, access personalized support, and receive immediate feedback. Yet speed is not synonymous with depth. When answers arrive instantly, the cognitive effort that builds understanding may be bypassed.

This chapter explores how AI is rewiring the structure of learning. It examines the tension between efficiency and intellectual development, between assistance and dependency. When AI tutors guide students step by step, the traditional struggle that once forged resilience and critical thinking may diminish. Struggle, though uncomfortable, has historically been a crucial part of growth.

As educational environments integrate AI more deeply, the definition of critical thinking itself is evolving. Students must now learn not only subject matter, but how to evaluate algorithmic outputs, question sources, and interpret generated information. The challenge is not whether AI belongs in education—it already does—but how to use it without eroding the very skills education is meant to strengthen.

Understanding this shift is essential, because the future of learning will determine the future of thought.

Learning Faster but Thinking Less

Artificial Intelligence has transformed education by dramatically increasing the speed at which information can be accessed, summarized, and applied. Students can now receive instant explanations, automated feedback, and fully structured responses to complex questions. On the surface, this appears to represent progress. Learning becomes efficient. Time is saved. Friction is reduced. Yet beneath this acceleration lies a critical tension: when learning becomes faster, thinking may become shallower.

Speed changes the cognitive experience of education. Traditional learning required effort—reading dense material, grappling with ambiguity, making mistakes, and revising understanding. These processes were not obstacles; they were integral to intellectual development. Struggle forced engagement. Engagement built comprehension. Comprehension enabled reasoning.

AI tools minimize that struggle. When a student encounters difficulty, a system can generate a summary, provide a step-by-step solution, or even produce a complete essay. The barrier between confusion and clarity narrows. While this support can be valuable, it risks bypassing the mental processes that lead to deep understanding. Instead of constructing knowledge, students may consume it.

The distinction between exposure and comprehension becomes blurred. A student who reads an AI-generated explanation may feel informed, but without wrestling with the material, the understanding may remain fragile. Thinking involves synthesis—connecting new ideas to existing frameworks. When learning is reduced to retrieval, synthesis weakens.

Another consequence is reduced tolerance for cognitive discomfort. Deep thinking often involves uncertainty. It requires holding multiple possibilities in mind and resisting premature closure. When answers are immediate, the mind becomes conditioned to expect resolution without delay. Patience diminishes. Complex problems feel frustrating rather than stimulating.

This shift affects attention as well. AI-generated summaries condense information into digestible fragments. While efficient, this format encourages surface-level engagement. Long-form reading and sustained analysis demand focus. If students increasingly rely on condensed outputs, the skill of deep reading may decline.

The impact extends beyond academic performance. Education is meant to cultivate independent reasoning. When students depend on AI for answers, they may lose confidence in their ability to think critically. The habit of seeking external validation replaces internal evaluation. Over time, thinking becomes reactive—triggered by prompts rather than initiated by curiosity.

Importantly, faster learning does not guarantee mastery. Mastery requires repetition, reflection, and application. AI can accelerate access to information, but it cannot internalize it for the learner. Without active engagement, knowledge remains external. The student knows how to obtain answers, but not necessarily how to generate them.

There is also a risk of intellectual complacency. When systems produce polished responses effortlessly, students may feel less motivated to refine their own ideas. The gap between machine-generated fluency and personal effort can discourage persistence. Instead of improving their skills, learners may rely on tools to compensate.

However, the issue is not speed itself, but imbalance. AI can enhance education when used to support deeper exploration. It can provide alternative explanations, simulate scenarios, and adapt to individual needs. The problem arises when efficiency replaces intellectual growth as the primary goal.

Educational systems must adapt thoughtfully. Teaching students how to use AI responsibly—questioning outputs, verifying sources, and integrating insights—becomes essential. Critical thinking in the age of AI involves evaluating both content and the systems that produce it.

Learning faster is not inherently detrimental. The danger lies in equating speed with understanding. Thinking requires time. It demands mental friction and sustained effort. When these elements are removed, intellectual development may stagnate.

The challenge for modern education is to harness AI's efficiency without sacrificing depth. Students must learn not only to access knowledge quickly, but to process it deliberately. The future of learning depends on preserving the value of thinking—even in a world where answers arrive instantly.

In the end, education is not measured by how quickly information is acquired, but by how deeply it is understood. AI can accelerate learning, but only human effort can transform information into wisdom.

AI Tutors and the Loss of Struggle

Artificial Intelligence has introduced a new educational companion: the AI tutor. Available at any hour, infinitely patient, and capable of generating personalized explanations in seconds, AI tutors promise to democratize learning. They can adapt to different skill levels, break down complex problems, and provide instant feedback. For many students, this feels like an unprecedented advantage. Yet embedded within this convenience is a critical concern—the gradual loss of productive struggle.

Struggle has historically been central to learning. When students confront difficulty, they are forced to think actively. They test assumptions, revise approaches, and confront gaps in understanding. This process strengthens cognitive resilience. It builds problem-solving skills and deep comprehension. Without friction, intellectual muscles do not develop.

AI tutors reduce friction dramatically. Faced with confusion, a student can request a step-by-step solution. Instead of grappling with uncertainty, they receive clarity almost immediately. While this may enhance short-term performance, it risks weakening long-term mastery. The mind learns to expect assistance rather than cultivate persistence.

The psychological impact is subtle but significant. Struggle fosters confidence. When students overcome challenges independently, they internalize a sense of capability. AI tutors can inadvertently undermine this process. If success is achieved primarily through external guidance, self-efficacy may decline. The student may feel capable only when supported by the system.

Another consequence is the erosion of metacognition—the ability to think about one's own thinking. Traditional learning involves reflecting on errors, identifying patterns of misunderstanding, and adjusting strategies.

When AI provides immediate correction, the opportunity for reflection narrows. The focus shifts from process to outcome.

AI tutors are particularly effective at procedural tasks—solving equations, explaining grammar, summarizing content. However, they cannot fully replicate the nuanced mentorship of a human educator. Human teachers perceive emotional cues, challenge students strategically, and cultivate curiosity. AI tutors, by contrast, optimize for clarity and engagement. They respond to prompts rather than initiate deeper exploration.

The loss of struggle also affects creativity. Creative breakthroughs often emerge from wrestling with ambiguity. When answers are too accessible, exploration diminishes. Students may settle for adequate solutions rather than pursuing original insight. The habit of experimentation weakens.

Importantly, not all struggle is beneficial. Excessive frustration can discourage learners. AI tutors can provide scaffolding that supports progress without overwhelming the student. The challenge lies in balance. When support replaces effort entirely, growth stagnates. When support guides but does not solve, learning flourishes.

There is also a social dimension to consider. Traditional learning environments foster collaboration, debate, and shared problem-solving. AI tutoring is often solitary. While personalized, it lacks the interpersonal dynamics that enrich understanding. Students may miss opportunities to learn from peers and develop communication skills.

Dependence on AI tutors can also alter assessment practices. If students rely heavily on generated explanations, distinguishing between assisted and independent work becomes difficult. Educational institutions must adapt evaluation methods to ensure genuine comprehension.

The presence of AI tutors demands a redefinition of academic integrity. Learning should not be measured solely by correct answers, but by the ability to reason through problems. Educators must teach students how to use AI responsibly—leveraging support while preserving ownership of thought.

Ultimately, the issue is not whether AI tutors should exist, but how they are integrated. When used thoughtfully, they can enhance accessibility and provide targeted assistance. When used uncritically, they risk diminishing the formative power of struggle.

Struggle is not an obstacle to learning; it is a pathway. It cultivates perseverance, curiosity, and depth. AI tutors can guide learners along this path, but they should not carry them to the destination.

In an age of intelligent assistance, preserving the value of effort is essential. Education must remain a process of growth, not merely a transaction of answers. The true measure of learning is not speed, but resilience—the capacity to think independently when guidance is absent.

What Critical Thinking Looks Like Now

Critical thinking has long been defined as the ability to analyze information, evaluate arguments, detect bias, and draw reasoned conclusions. In a world shaped by Artificial Intelligence, however, the nature of critical thinking is evolving. It is no longer sufficient to assess texts, speeches, or data alone. Modern critical thinking must also evaluate the systems that generate and filter information. It must account for algorithmic mediation, data bias, and automated outputs.

In previous eras, critical thinking focused primarily on content. A student examined the credibility of a source, the logic of an argument, or the strength of evidence. Today, much of the content encountered is curated, summarized, or generated by AI systems. This introduces a new layer of complexity. The question is no longer just "Is this information accurate?" but also "How was this information produced, and by whom?"

Critical thinking now requires algorithmic literacy. Individuals must understand that search results are ranked, feeds are personalized, and recommendations are optimized for engagement. Awareness of these mechanisms allows for more deliberate engagement. Without such awareness, individuals may mistake curated content for comprehensive truth.

Another transformation involves the evaluation of AI-generated material. Language models can produce coherent essays, summaries, and analyses. These outputs may appear authoritative, yet they are based on probabilistic patterns rather than understanding. Critical thinkers must verify claims, cross-check sources, and assess context. The fluency of an answer does not guarantee its accuracy.

The speed of information also challenges critical thinking. AI accelerates access to knowledge, reducing the time between question and answer. This can discourage reflection. True critical thinking requires pause—time to consider alternatives, question assumptions, and recognize uncertainty. In an environment optimized for immediacy, cultivating deliberate thought becomes an intentional practice.

Moreover, critical thinking now involves recognizing bias not only in human narratives but in algorithmic systems. Data reflects historical patterns, and those patterns may encode inequality. Evaluating fairness requires examining both input data and system objectives. Understanding that intelligence can be structured around specific goals—such as engagement or profit—adds depth to analysis.

The social dimension of critical thinking has also shifted. AI-driven platforms amplify certain perspectives while marginalizing others. Exposure to information is often filtered through personalized algorithms. Critical thinkers must actively seek diverse viewpoints rather than rely solely on what appears in their feed. Intellectual independence requires stepping beyond curated environments.

In education, this evolution demands new skills. Students must learn to collaborate with AI without surrendering reasoning. They must treat AI as a tool for exploration rather than a substitute for thought. Asking deeper questions—"Why is this answer structured this way?" "What assumptions underlie this response?"—becomes essential.

Importantly, critical thinking now includes self-awareness. Individuals must examine how algorithms influence their preferences and beliefs. Recognizing the subtle ways in which repeated exposure shapes perception is part of intellectual maturity. Awareness of one's own cognitive biases is no longer sufficient; awareness of technological mediation is equally necessary.

Ethical reflection is another emerging component. Decisions influenced by AI often involve moral considerations. Evaluating outcomes requires balancing efficiency with fairness, accuracy with privacy, and innovation with accountability. Critical thinking extends beyond logic to include values.

Despite these changes, the core of critical thinking remains human. It involves curiosity, skepticism, and a willingness to question authority—whether that authority is institutional or algorithmic. The presence of AI does not diminish the importance of these qualities; it intensifies them.

In many ways, critical thinking today is more demanding than ever. The volume of information is vast, the sources are diverse, and the systems that mediate access are complex. Navigating this environment requires intellectual discipline.

The future of learning depends on adapting critical thinking to this new landscape. Rather than resisting AI, learners must engage with it consciously. They must verify, contextualize, and interpret.

What critical thinking looks like now is not rejection of technology, but partnership with scrutiny. It is the ability to question both content and code, both narrative and algorithm. In an AI-guided world, the preservation of independent thought depends on expanding critical thinking—not abandoning it.

Chapter 10: Identity, Self-Worth, and Human Relevance

Artificial Intelligence is no longer confined to mechanical tasks. It writes, designs, analyzes, predicts, composes, and optimizes. As machines begin to perform activities once considered uniquely human, a deeper psychological question emerges: What does this mean for identity and self-worth? When intelligence is no longer exclusively human, the definition of human value begins to shift.

For centuries, skill and productivity have been central to personal identity. A person's profession, creativity, or expertise often shaped how they saw themselves and how they were perceived by others. AI challenges this foundation. When systems can generate text in seconds, analyze data with precision, and perform tasks at scale, comparison becomes unavoidable. Humans may begin measuring their abilities against machines designed for efficiency rather than meaning.

This comparison is not merely economic—it is existential. Productivity has become a cultural benchmark for value. If machines outperform humans in speed and accuracy, individuals may question their relevance. The fear of obsolescence extends beyond job markets into personal identity. What remains uniquely human in a world of accelerating automation?

This chapter explores the psychological and cultural consequences of living alongside intelligent systems. It examines how self-worth is influenced by comparison, how definitions of productivity shape identity, and how individuals respond to being outperformed by machines. The challenge is not simply adapting to new tools, but redefining value in a way that preserves dignity and meaning.

Understanding this shift is essential, because technological progress does not merely change industries—it reshapes how humans see themselves.

Measuring Ourselves Against Machines

Artificial Intelligence has introduced a new and subtle psychological tension into modern life: comparison. For centuries, humans compared themselves primarily to other humans—peers, colleagues, competitors. Today, many individuals find themselves measuring their abilities against machines. This shift alters not only professional dynamics but personal identity. When machines write faster, calculate more accurately, and process information at scale, the instinct to compare becomes unavoidable.

Comparison begins in productivity. AI systems complete tasks in seconds that once required hours. They generate structured reports, summarize complex research, and draft creative content with remarkable speed. In professional environments where efficiency is valued, this performance can create pressure. Workers may feel slower, less capable, or replaceable by comparison. The machine becomes a benchmark, even though it was never meant to serve as a human standard.

The problem lies in misunderstanding the nature of machine capability. AI systems are optimized for specific tasks within defined parameters. They process patterns based on vast datasets. Humans, by contrast, bring context, emotion, ethics, and lived experience to their work. Yet in cultures that prioritize measurable output, these qualitative dimensions are often undervalued. Speed and scale overshadow nuance.

Measuring ourselves against machines can distort self-perception. When individuals focus on areas where machines excel—calculation, repetition, data retrieval—they may overlook uniquely human strengths. Creativity rooted in personal experience, empathy, moral reasoning, and adaptability cannot be reduced to computational performance. However, because machine output appears polished and precise, it can trigger feelings of inadequacy.

This comparison is reinforced by media narratives that celebrate technological superiority. Headlines frequently emphasize AI outperforming humans in specific tasks. While often accurate within narrow domains, such comparisons rarely capture the broader context of human complexity. Nevertheless, the psychological impact persists. The idea of being "outperformed" challenges pride and confidence.

The workplace intensifies this tension. As organizations adopt AI tools to increase efficiency, employees may perceive their roles as threatened. Even when AI functions as assistance rather than replacement, the perception of substitution can affect morale. Individuals may question their long-term relevance. This uncertainty can erode intrinsic motivation.

Comparison also affects creative fields. Writers, designers, and musicians may see AI-generated outputs that rival professional quality. The machine's fluency can feel intimidating. Yet these outputs are based on recombination of existing patterns, not lived expression. Human creativity is shaped by memory, emotion, and intention. Machines simulate style; humans generate meaning.

Social comparison theory suggests that individuals evaluate themselves relative to perceived standards. When machines become part of that reference framework, standards shift toward optimization. Humans may feel compelled to match algorithmic efficiency, working longer hours or accelerating output to compete. This dynamic risks burnout and diminished well-being.

Another dimension of comparison involves cognitive ability. AI's capacity to process large volumes of information challenges traditional notions of intelligence. Historically, intelligence was associated with memory and calculation. As machines excel in these domains, definitions of intelligence evolve. Humans may begin to value different attributes—critical thinking, ethical reasoning, emotional intelligence—precisely because machines cannot replicate them fully.

Importantly, measuring ourselves against machines can obscure a fundamental truth: machines are tools. They are designed to extend human capability, not to redefine human worth. When comparison shifts from utility to identity, the relationship becomes unhealthy. The purpose of AI is augmentation, not competition.

There is also a danger in internalizing machine standards. Productivity metrics optimized for algorithms may not align with human rhythms. Creativity, insight, and emotional labor require time and reflection. Measuring these processes against instantaneous outputs diminishes their value.

Preserving self-worth in an AI-driven world requires reframing comparison. Instead of asking whether humans outperform machines, the question becomes how machines support human potential. Collaboration replaces competition. Machines handle repetitive or data-intensive tasks, freeing humans to focus on judgment, empathy, and innovation.

The psychological challenge is to resist equating speed with superiority. Human relevance is not defined by efficiency alone. It is defined by meaning, connection, and moral agency. Measuring ourselves against machines may be inevitable, but redefining the metrics of value is essential.

In the end, the goal is not to outperform machines, but to integrate them responsibly. Humans remain authors of purpose. Machines execute processes. When comparison shifts from rivalry to partnership, self-worth can remain intact—even in the presence of extraordinary technological capability.

Productivity, Value, and Human Obsolescence

Modern society has long equated productivity with value. From industrial labor to knowledge work, output has been a primary measure of worth. How much can be produced? How efficiently can tasks be completed? How consistently can performance be optimized? In an age shaped by Artificial Intelligence, these questions intensify. As machines outperform humans in speed, accuracy, and scale, the relationship between productivity and value is being fundamentally challenged.

Artificial Intelligence excels at tasks defined by repetition, data analysis, and structured logic. It processes information tirelessly and performs calculations at speeds unattainable by humans. In industries driven by metrics—finance, logistics, customer service, manufacturing—AI often enhances efficiency dramatically. This technological acceleration reinforces a cultural narrative: productivity is paramount.

However, when productivity becomes the central metric of value, human identity is placed at risk. If machines can produce more in less time, what distinguishes human contribution? The fear of obsolescence arises not only from job displacement but from perceived redundancy. When roles once defined by expertise are automated, individuals may question their relevance.

This concern is amplified by economic structures. In competitive markets, organizations adopt AI to reduce costs and maximize output. Workers observe these shifts and interpret them through a lens of replaceability. Even when AI functions as augmentation rather than replacement, the perception of competition persists. Productivity comparisons become personal.

Yet equating human value solely with measurable output oversimplifies the complexity of human contribution. Humans bring qualities that extend beyond efficiency—empathy, ethical reasoning, creativity rooted in lived experience, and the capacity for moral judgment. These attributes do not lend themselves easily to quantification, and thus may be undervalued in productivity-driven systems.

The concept of human obsolescence reflects a deeper philosophical tension. Throughout history, technological advancements have displaced certain forms of labor while creating new ones. The agricultural revolution reduced the need for manual farming labor. The industrial revolution automated manufacturing. In each case, society adapted. However, AI differs in scope. It encroaches not only on physical tasks but on cognitive ones. This breadth intensifies anxiety.

Productivity metrics also shape self-worth. Many individuals derive identity from professional competence. When AI systems perform similar tasks more efficiently, confidence may erode. The narrative of "being outperformed" can lead to insecurity and diminished motivation. Productivity becomes a comparative benchmark rather than a personal standard.

The cultural obsession with optimization compounds this dynamic. Algorithms prioritize speed and scale. Human processes—reflection, collaboration, emotional labor—are slower by nature. When organizational cultures adopt algorithmic standards, human rhythms may feel inadequate. Burnout becomes more likely as individuals attempt to match machine-level output.

However, framing AI as a rival overlooks its intended role as a tool.

Machines are designed to enhance human capability, not to define human worth. The risk lies in allowing economic incentives to redefine value solely through efficiency. When productivity becomes the dominant criterion, other dimensions of contribution—care, mentorship, ethical leadership—are marginalized.

Redefining value requires expanding metrics beyond output. Human relevance cannot be measured solely in units of production. Meaningful work involves context, purpose, and relational impact. A teacher's influence, a caregiver's compassion, or an artist's expression cannot be captured by speed alone.

The fear of obsolescence also reveals an opportunity for recalibration. As AI assumes repetitive and data-intensive tasks, humans may be freed to focus on roles that emphasize judgment, empathy, and innovation. Rather than competing with machines, individuals can leverage them to amplify uniquely human strengths.

Societal structures must adapt accordingly. Education systems should prioritize critical thinking, ethical reasoning, and creativity—skills less susceptible to automation. Organizations must recognize that sustainable progress depends on integrating human insight with technological efficiency.

Human obsolescence is not an inevitable outcome of technological advancement. It is a narrative shaped by how society defines value. If productivity remains the sole measure, comparison with machines will feel threatening. If value encompasses meaning, connection, and ethical agency, human relevance endures.

Ultimately, AI challenges not human capability, but human definition. The question is not whether machines can produce more—they can—but whether productivity alone should determine worth. Preserving human dignity in an AI-driven world requires redefining value in terms that machines cannot replicate: consciousness, compassion, and purpose.

Psychological Impact of Being "Outperformed"

Throughout history, competition has largely existed between humans. Individuals compared themselves to peers—colleagues, classmates, rivals. Success and failure were measured within shared human limitations. Artificial Intelligence introduces a fundamentally different form of comparison. When machines outperform humans in speed, memory, calculation, and even certain creative tasks, the psychological landscape shifts. The experience of being "outperformed" by a non-human system carries unique emotional consequences.

One immediate reaction is diminished self-efficacy. Self-efficacy refers to a person's belief in their own ability to succeed. When individuals repeatedly observe machines completing tasks more efficiently, they may begin to question their competence. Even if the task is narrow or technical, the perception of inferiority can generalize. Confidence declines not because skills disappear, but because standards change.

Another psychological response is identity destabilization. Many people define themselves through their expertise. A writer values linguistic fluency. An analyst values numerical precision. When AI demonstrates similar capabilities at scale, the foundation of identity feels threatened. The comparison is not only about output; it is about meaning. If a machine can do what I do faster and with fewer errors, what distinguishes me?

This tension can lead to anxiety and anticipatory stress. The fear of replacement—whether realistic or exaggerated—creates uncertainty. Workers may worry about job security. Students may worry about future relevance. This uncertainty affects motivation and mental well-being. The stress is often diffuse, not tied to a specific event but to a broader cultural narrative of technological dominance.

Social comparison theory helps explain this phenomenon. Humans naturally evaluate themselves relative to others. When the "other" becomes a machine optimized for performance, the comparison becomes skewed. Machines do not experience fatigue, distraction, or emotional fluctuation. They operate within parameters designed for efficiency. Comparing human performance to machine output ignores these fundamental differences, yet the comparison persists.

There is also the risk of learned helplessness. If individuals perceive that no matter how much effort they invest, machines will outperform them, they may reduce effort altogether. Motivation declines. Innovation slows. This response is not inevitable, but it can emerge in environments where algorithmic superiority is emphasized without context.

In creative fields, the psychological impact may be particularly complex. Seeing AI generate poetry, artwork, or music can evoke both admiration and insecurity. Creators may question the uniqueness of their voice. Yet creativity rooted in lived experience, emotion, and personal narrative remains distinct. The tension arises when machine-generated outputs are evaluated solely by surface quality rather than depth of meaning.

The feeling of being outperformed can also affect interpersonal dynamics. If organizations prioritize machine efficiency over human development, employees may feel undervalued. Morale declines when contributions are measured against algorithmic standards rather than human potential. Over time, workplace culture may shift toward performance anxiety rather than collaboration.

However, being outperformed does not necessarily equate to being obsolete. Human history demonstrates adaptation. When calculators replaced manual arithmetic, mathematicians did not disappear. Instead, their focus shifted to higher-level reasoning. Similarly, AI can assume routine cognitive tasks while humans concentrate on interpretation, ethics, and strategy.

Reframing comparison is crucial. Machines are tools optimized for specific functions. Humans possess consciousness, empathy, moral judgment, and contextual understanding. The psychological harm arises when comparison is framed as competition rather than augmentation. If AI is viewed as an extension of capability rather than a rival, the narrative changes.

Educational systems and organizations play a role in shaping this narrative. Emphasizing uniquely human strengths—critical thinking, emotional intelligence, adaptability—can mitigate feelings of inadequacy. Encouraging collaboration between human and machine fosters empowerment rather than fear.

Ultimately, the psychological impact of being outperformed reflects deeper questions about value. If worth is defined purely by speed and output, comparison with machines will feel threatening. If worth includes creativity, compassion, and ethical agency, the comparison loses its sting.

The presence of AI challenges humans to redefine excellence. Being outperformed in narrow domains does not diminish humanity. Instead, it invites reflection on what cannot be automated. Preserving mental resilience in an AI-driven world requires shifting from rivalry to partnership—recognizing that performance is only one dimension of human significance.

Chapter 11: Moral Reasoning in a Machine-Mediated World

Artificial Intelligence is no longer limited to technical calculations or routine automation. It increasingly participates in decisions that carry moral weight—who receives a loan, which content is removed, how medical resources are allocated, or how risks are assessed. As algorithms become embedded in systems of governance, commerce, and communication, they influence choices that shape human lives. This evolution raises a profound question: What happens to moral reasoning when machines mediate our decisions?

Traditionally, ethics has been a human responsibility. Moral judgment involves empathy, contextual awareness, and the capacity to weigh competing values. It requires not only logic but conscience. AI systems, however, operate on predefined objectives and statistical models. They optimize for efficiency, accuracy, or engagement, but they do not possess moral understanding. When such systems guide outcomes, ethical considerations may be reduced to measurable proxies.

This chapter explores the consequences of delegating ethical decisions to algorithms. It examines how responsibility becomes diffused when outcomes are attributed to "the system" rather than to individuals or institutions. When a machine produces a recommendation, accountability can become obscured. Yet the moral impact remains real.

As AI increasingly shapes perceptions of fairness and legitimacy, it also influences how society defines right and wrong. Decisions mediated by machines may appear neutral, even when they embed value judgments. Understanding this shift is essential, because technology does not eliminate moral responsibility—it redistributes it. In a machine-mediated world, preserving ethical clarity requires conscious oversight, transparency, and human engagement.

Delegating Ethics to Algorithms

As Artificial Intelligence becomes more deeply embedded in social systems, it is increasingly tasked with decisions that carry moral weight. Algorithms determine which content is removed from platforms, how creditworthiness is assessed, which job applicants are shortlisted, and even how medical resources are prioritized. In these contexts, ethical judgment is no longer exercised solely by humans—it is encoded into systems. This shift raises a critical concern: what happens when ethics is delegated to algorithms?

Delegating ethics does not necessarily mean abandoning moral responsibility outright. Rather, it involves translating ethical principles into computational rules. Developers attempt to define fairness, safety, and harm in measurable terms. These definitions are embedded into models that optimize for specified objectives. However, ethical reasoning is rarely reducible to fixed criteria. It involves context, empathy, and the ability to weigh competing values.

Algorithms operate through predefined parameters. They assess inputs based on training data and programmed constraints. While they may approximate fairness statistically, they cannot comprehend moral nuance. For example, a content moderation system may remove posts based on keyword detection or probability scores. Yet context matters—satire, academic discussion, or cultural expression may be misinterpreted. Delegating moderation to algorithms risks flattening complexity.

One challenge lies in defining ethical metrics. Concepts such as fairness, equality, and justice are deeply contested. When developers operationalize these values into algorithms, they make interpretive choices. Should fairness mean equal outcomes or equal opportunities? Should risk assessment prioritize minimizing false positives or false negatives? These decisions reflect philosophical positions, even if framed technically.

Delegation also diffuses accountability. When an algorithm denies a loan or flags a user, responsibility may appear to reside with the system. Individuals within organizations may defer to the algorithm's output, believing it to be objective. This diffusion can weaken ethical scrutiny. If harm occurs, identifying responsibility becomes difficult. The algorithm is not a moral agent, yet it shapes outcomes.

The appeal of delegating ethics stems from a desire for consistency. Human decision-making can be inconsistent, influenced by mood, bias, or fatigue. Algorithms promise standardized application of rules. In theory, this reduces arbitrariness. In practice, however, consistency does not guarantee justice. If underlying criteria are flawed or biased, consistent application amplifies harm.

Another dimension involves scale. Human ethical review is limited by time and capacity. Algorithms operate at scale, processing thousands or millions of cases rapidly. This scalability is attractive in large systems, such as social media platforms. Yet scaling ethical decisions magnifies the impact of errors. A miscalibrated model can affect vast populations.

Delegating ethics also alters perception. When decisions are attributed to algorithms, they may appear impartial. This perception can legitimize outcomes, even when they embed subjective assumptions. The authority of technology shields value judgments behind technical language.

Importantly, AI systems cannot feel empathy. Ethical reasoning in humans involves emotional awareness and moral imagination. It requires considering the lived experience of those affected. Algorithms simulate evaluation through data patterns. They cannot experience harm or injustice. This absence of moral consciousness limits their capacity to adjudicate complex dilemmas.

However, rejecting algorithmic involvement entirely may not be feasible. In large systems, AI can assist in identifying patterns of discrimination or harmful behavior more effectively than humans alone. The issue is not whether algorithms should play a role, but how that role is structured.

Human oversight is essential. Ethical delegation must be accompanied by transparency, auditability, and avenues for appeal. Systems should be designed to support, not replace, human judgment. Decision-making frameworks must remain accountable to societal values.

Delegating ethics to algorithms reflects a broader cultural shift toward technological authority. As systems become more sophisticated, the temptation to rely on them increases. Yet moral responsibility cannot be outsourced fully. Algorithms execute defined objectives; they do not determine moral purpose.

In a machine-mediated world, preserving ethical integrity requires recognizing the limits of computation. Ethical reasoning demands interpretation, reflection, and empathy—qualities that remain distinctly human. Algorithms may assist in applying principles, but defining and revising those principles remains a human responsibility.

Ultimately, delegating ethics to algorithms challenges society to confront how values are translated into code. Without careful governance, the promise of efficiency may overshadow the complexity of justice. The future of moral reasoning depends on ensuring that machines serve ethical frameworks, rather than silently redefining them.

Responsibility Without Accountability

As Artificial Intelligence systems increasingly mediate decisions that affect human lives, a troubling dynamic emerges: responsibility without accountability. Outcomes occur. Decisions are made. Consequences unfold. Yet when harm arises, identifying who is responsible becomes complex. The algorithm acted. The organization implemented it. The developer designed it. The user followed its output. In this distributed chain, accountability can dissolve.

Traditionally, responsibility is tied to agency. A person makes a decision and bears the moral and legal consequences. AI disrupts this model. Algorithms generate recommendations or classifications that influence actions, but they are not moral agents. They cannot intend harm, feel remorse, or be punished. Yet their outputs shape real-world outcomes.

When a system denies a loan, flags a suspect, or removes content, individuals often attribute the decision to "the algorithm." This phrasing distances responsibility from human actors. It suggests inevitability—an automated process rather than a deliberate choice. Organizational leaders may defer to technical explanations. Employees may claim compliance with system outputs. Accountability becomes diffuse.

This diffusion is reinforced by complexity. Modern AI systems are built through layers of data collection, model training, parameter tuning, and deployment. Multiple teams contribute. Vendors provide components. Policies guide implementation. In such ecosystems, pinpointing responsibility is challenging. Each actor may claim limited control.

The problem is compounded by opacity. Many AI systems function as black boxes, particularly those based on deep learning. Their internal decision pathways are difficult to interpret. When an outcome appears biased or harmful, explaining how it occurred may be technically complex. Without transparency, accountability weakens.

Responsibility without accountability also manifests in design choices. Developers embed assumptions into models—defining success metrics, selecting training data, calibrating thresholds. These decisions influence outcomes. Yet once deployed, the system's outputs may be treated as objective facts. The human decisions that shaped the model fade from view.

Organizations often emphasize performance metrics—accuracy, efficiency, scalability—over ethical evaluation. When systems meet technical benchmarks, ethical scrutiny may diminish. If harm occurs, companies may attribute it to unintended side effects or data limitations. The structural incentives prioritize innovation speed over accountability mechanisms.

The legal framework surrounding AI is still evolving. In many jurisdictions, existing laws were not designed for algorithmic mediation. Liability may be unclear. Should responsibility fall on developers, deployers, data providers, or users? Without clear standards, accountability gaps persist.

This ambiguity has psychological consequences. Individuals affected by algorithmic decisions may feel powerless. Appeals processes may be opaque or nonexistent. When explanations are unavailable, trust erodes. Responsibility seems abstract, unaddressable.

The notion of responsibility without accountability also affects moral culture. When decision-making is mediated by systems, individuals may feel less personally responsible. A hiring manager may rely on algorithmic screening rather than exercising judgment. A content moderator may defer to automated flags. Over time, moral engagement diminishes.

However, accountability is not impossible in AI systems—it requires intentional design. Transparency mechanisms, audit trails, and explainability features can illuminate decision processes. Clear governance structures can define roles and responsibilities. Ethical oversight committees can monitor deployment and address grievances.

Crucially, organizations must resist the temptation to treat AI as an autonomous authority. Systems execute objectives defined by humans. Responsibility ultimately resides with those who design, deploy, and maintain them. Accountability frameworks must reflect this reality.

Public policy also plays a role. Regulatory standards can mandate transparency, fairness audits, and redress mechanisms. Clear liability guidelines can ensure that harms are addressed rather than dismissed as technical anomalies.

Responsibility without accountability undermines trust. As AI becomes embedded in critical domains—finance, healthcare, justice—society must ensure that decisions remain accountable to human values. Diffused responsibility cannot become an excuse for ethical evasion.

The challenge is cultural as well as technical. Leaders must cultivate environments where questioning algorithmic outputs is encouraged. Employees must feel empowered to override systems when ethical concerns arise. Accountability must be proactive, not reactive.

In a machine-mediated world, responsibility cannot vanish into code. Algorithms may calculate, but humans remain accountable. Ensuring that accountability accompanies technological advancement is essential to preserving fairness, trust, and moral integrity.

When Machines Influence Right and Wrong

Artificial Intelligence increasingly participates in decisions that shape perceptions of morality. While machines do not possess conscience or moral awareness, they influence what individuals see, how they interpret events, and which actions are rewarded or penalized. Over time, this influence can subtly affect collective notions of right and wrong. The question is not whether machines have moral judgment—they do not—but how their design and deployment shape human moral reasoning.

AI systems curate information at scale. Social media algorithms determine which posts gain visibility, which narratives trend, and which perspectives fade. If engagement metrics prioritize emotionally charged or divisive content, public discourse may shift toward polarization. What becomes widely visible can feel legitimate. Moral norms are reinforced through repetition and amplification.

Content moderation systems also participate in moral boundary-setting. By removing certain material or flagging speech, algorithms help define acceptable behavior. While these systems are guided by policies created by humans, their automated enforcement can appear neutral and authoritative. Users may internalize these boundaries as objective standards, even though they reflect institutional choices.

Recommendation systems shape values indirectly. When platforms promote specific products, lifestyles, or cultural ideals, they influence aspirations and self-perception. Repeated exposure normalizes certain behaviors. Over time, algorithmic curation can redefine what is perceived as desirable or appropriate.

In high-stakes domains, AI's moral influence becomes more explicit. Predictive policing systems may guide law enforcement priorities. Risk assessment tools may influence sentencing decisions. Medical triage algorithms may determine resource allocation. Although these systems rely on statistical models, their outputs carry ethical implications. Decisions about risk tolerance, false positives, and acceptable trade-offs embed moral judgments within technical frameworks.

The challenge lies in the translation of ethical principles into computational objectives. Concepts such as fairness, harm reduction, and equity are complex and context-dependent. When encoded into algorithms, they are simplified into measurable criteria. This simplification may omit nuance. The system executes predefined rules, but moral life often requires flexibility and interpretation.

Machines influence right and wrong through feedback loops. Behaviors that generate engagement are amplified. Users adapt to algorithmic incentives. If provocative content receives visibility, individuals may adjust expression accordingly. Moral discourse becomes shaped by platform dynamics rather than deliberate ethical reflection.

Another dimension involves the perception of authority. When algorithmic decisions appear objective, individuals may accept them without scrutiny. If a system labels content as misinformation or assigns a risk score, it can shape belief formation. The authority of data can overshadow individual moral reasoning.

Importantly, machines do not originate moral values. They reflect the priorities embedded by designers, organizations, and governing bodies. However, because their influence operates at scale and often invisibly, the effects can be profound. Ethical norms may evolve in response to algorithmic structures rather than collective deliberation.

This dynamic raises concerns about democratic accountability. If private corporations control algorithms that influence moral discourse, power over normative boundaries becomes centralized. Decisions about what is amplified or suppressed affect public understanding of justice, fairness, and truth.

Despite these risks, AI can also support ethical progress. Algorithms can identify discriminatory patterns, detect harmful behavior, and promote inclusive practices. The influence of machines on morality is not inherently negative. It depends on governance, transparency; and the values guiding design.

Preserving moral agency requires awareness. Individuals must recognize that algorithmic outputs are not moral truths, but reflections of programmed objectives. Critical engagement with technology is essential to prevent passive acceptance.

Ultimately, right and wrong are human concepts grounded in empathy, experience, and collective reasoning. Machines can assist in applying ethical frameworks, but they cannot define them. When machines influence moral perception, responsibility remains human.

In a machine-mediated world, ethical clarity depends on conscious oversight. Society must ensure that algorithms serve moral principles rather than silently reshape them. The future of moral reasoning will not be determined by machines alone, but by how humans choose to guide and question the intelligence they create.

Chapter 12:
The Future of Human Thought

Artificial Intelligence is not merely a technological development; it is a cognitive force. It influences how we learn, decide, create, remember, and relate. As AI systems become increasingly integrated into daily life, a deeper question emerges: What is happening to human thought itself? Are we witnessing the evolution of cognition through augmentation, or the gradual decline of independent reasoning?

Throughout history, tools have reshaped thinking. Writing externalized memory. The printing press expanded access to knowledge. The internet accelerated information exchange. Each transformation sparked concern about intellectual decline, yet also enabled new forms of creativity and analysis. AI represents a more profound shift because it does not simply store or transmit information—it processes, predicts, and generates it. In doing so, it participates directly in cognitive tasks once considered uniquely human.

This chapter explores the long-term trajectory of human thought in an AI-saturated world. Will collaboration with intelligent systems elevate reasoning and creativity, or will dependence diminish depth and autonomy? As machines increasingly anticipate needs and provide solutions, the boundary between assistance and replacement becomes uncertain.

The central challenge is agency. Human thought is not defined solely by speed or efficiency, but by intention, reflection, and moral awareness. Preserving these qualities requires conscious engagement with technology rather than passive reliance.

The future of human thought will not be determined by AI alone, but by how humanity chooses to integrate it. Whether this era marks cognitive evolution or quiet erosion depends on the values, systems, and habits we cultivate moving forward.

Cognitive Evolution or Cognitive Decline

The integration of Artificial Intelligence into daily life raises a fundamental question about the trajectory of human cognition. Are we entering a phase of cognitive evolution—where machines amplify human capability—or are we witnessing the early signs of cognitive decline, where reliance erodes independent thought? The answer is neither simple nor singular. It depends not only on what AI can do, but on how humans choose to use it.

Throughout history, technological tools have reshaped cognition. The invention of writing externalized memory, allowing humans to record and transmit knowledge beyond the limits of recall. The printing press democratized access to information. Calculators reduced the need for manual computation. In each case, certain skills diminished while others expanded. The brain adapted. Cognitive evolution did not eliminate thinking—it redirected it.

Artificial Intelligence differs in scope. Unlike previous tools, AI does not merely store or calculate information; it interprets, predicts, and generates. It can summarize complex texts, propose solutions, and create content that resembles human reasoning. This shift moves technology from supporting cognition to participating in it. The boundary between tool and thinker becomes less distinct.

Cognitive evolution would imply that AI enhances higher-order thinking. By automating repetitive or data-intensive tasks, humans could redirect energy toward creativity, strategic reasoning, and ethical reflection. Freed from routine processing, the mind might engage more deeply with abstract concepts. AI could function as an intellectual collaborator, expanding problem-solving capacity.

There is evidence supporting this potential. Professionals use AI to analyze vast datasets, identify patterns, and generate insights that would otherwise be inaccessible. Students can explore alternative explanations and simulate scenarios that deepen understanding. In such contexts, AI serves as augmentation—a catalyst for expanded cognition.

However, cognitive decline is a parallel risk. When AI provides instant answers, the incentive to wrestle with complexity diminishes. Struggle, which strengthens neural pathways and deepens comprehension, may be bypassed. If individuals habitually outsource analysis, memory, and synthesis, cognitive skills may atrophy.

One area of concern is attention. AI systems often deliver condensed summaries and rapid responses. While efficient, this format can reduce tolerance for sustained focus. Deep reading and extended reasoning require patience. If cognitive habits shift toward brevity and immediacy, depth may suffer.

Memory is another dimension. Reliance on digital retrieval reduces the need for internal recall. While external memory systems have long existed, AI's predictive capabilities make information retrieval seamless. The brain may prioritize knowing how to access knowledge rather than retaining it. Whether this represents adaptation or erosion remains debated.

Critical thinking also faces transformation. When AI-generated outputs appear coherent and authoritative, individuals may accept them without scrutiny. If evaluation skills decline, cognitive independence weakens. Conversely, learning to question algorithmic outputs could strengthen analytical awareness. The outcome depends on education and cultural norms.

Cognitive evolution requires intentional engagement. If AI is treated as a partner in reasoning—its outputs examined, refined, and challenged—human cognition may expand. If treated as a substitute, passive consumption may replace active thought.

The concept of decline assumes that previous cognitive forms were ideal. Yet cognition has always evolved in response to environment. Oral cultures developed extraordinary memory. Literate societies emphasized analytical abstraction. The digital age fostered multitasking and networked thinking. AI may produce a new cognitive style—collaborative, iterative, and system-aware.

The challenge lies in preserving agency. Evolution implies growth in capacity and complexity. Decline implies diminished autonomy and skill. The difference hinges on whether humans remain intentional thinkers or become dependent operators.

Societal structures will influence this trajectory. Education must emphasize deep reasoning, not just tool proficiency. Workplaces must value human judgment alongside efficiency. Cultural narratives must resist equating speed with intelligence.

Ultimately, AI does not dictate cognitive destiny. It presents possibilities. Cognitive evolution and decline are not predetermined outcomes but potential paths. The human brain remains adaptable. The question is how it will adapt in an environment where thinking is increasingly shared with machines.

If humans cultivate awareness, reflection, and ethical discernment, AI may expand intellectual horizons. If convenience overrides engagement, cognitive erosion may follow. The future of human thought depends less on technological capability than on collective choice.

Coexistence or Quiet Replacement

As Artificial Intelligence advances across industries, education, creativity, and decision-making, society confronts a pivotal question: Are humans and machines moving toward coexistence, or is a quiet replacement already underway? The distinction is subtle. Replacement does not always arrive dramatically. It can occur gradually, through automation of tasks, shifting expectations, and evolving norms—until human presence becomes secondary rather than central.

Coexistence implies partnership. In this model, AI augments human capability. Machines handle repetitive, data-intensive, or high-speed tasks, freeing humans to focus on judgment, creativity, empathy, and ethical reasoning. Collaboration becomes the framework. The human defines goals; the machine executes processes. The relationship is complementary.

Quiet replacement, by contrast, unfolds incrementally. It begins when efficiency becomes the dominant priority. If a machine performs a task faster and cheaper, organizations adopt it. Human roles shift. Over time, certain functions become fully automated. Individuals may not notice the transition immediately. What was once a human responsibility becomes background infrastructure.

Replacement is not limited to employment. It can occur cognitively and socially. When AI systems generate written communication, compose music, or curate experiences, human contribution may diminish in visibility. If users become accustomed to machine-generated content, expectations adjust. Authentic human effort may feel slower or less polished by comparison.

The danger of quiet replacement lies in normalization. As automation expands, humans may gradually relinquish areas of responsibility. Decision-making may default to algorithmic outputs. Creative tasks may begin with machine drafts rather than personal exploration. Dependency increases subtly, often justified by convenience.

However, replacement is not inevitable. Human qualities remain distinct. Machines process patterns; humans assign meaning. AI can generate options, but it does not possess intention or moral awareness. These uniquely human dimensions anchor coexistence.

The economic dimension complicates the picture. In competitive markets, cost reduction drives automation. Organizations may prioritize machine performance over human employment. This structural pressure can accelerate replacement. Yet long-term sustainability depends on integrating human insight. Pure automation may lack adaptability in unpredictable contexts.

Psychologically, coexistence requires reframing identity. Humans must see AI not as a rival, but as an instrument. This shift reduces fear and fosters collaboration. If individuals define value solely through tasks that machines perform well, replacement feels threatening. If value includes empathy, ethical judgment, and creative depth, coexistence becomes viable.

Education plays a central role. Preparing individuals to work alongside AI rather than compete with it fosters resilience. Skills such as critical thinking, complex problem-solving, and emotional intelligence become foundational. Coexistence thrives when humans cultivate strengths machines cannot replicate fully.

There is also a governance dimension. Policies that encourage responsible integration—balancing innovation with labor protection—can mitigate abrupt displacement. Transparent oversight ensures that automation aligns with societal well-being rather than narrow economic incentives.

Quiet replacement often emerges where awareness is absent. When individuals do not question how systems reshape roles, transitions occur unnoticed. Recognizing incremental shifts is essential to maintaining agency.

Culturally, narratives about AI influence outcomes. If society frames technology as a tool for empowerment, coexistence gains momentum. If framed as inevitable superiority, resignation may follow. Perception shapes adaptation.

Importantly, coexistence does not mean stagnation. It involves redefining human roles in response to technological capability. Throughout history, humans have adapted to new tools by expanding domains of creativity and thought. The challenge with AI lies in its breadth—it touches cognitive domains previously reserved for humans.

The question is not whether machines will replace some tasks—they already have—but whether they will replace the human presence that gives those tasks meaning. Coexistence preserves that presence. Replacement diminishes it.

Ultimately, the path forward depends on intentional design and collective choice. If AI remains aligned with human values and oversight, partnership can flourish. If efficiency eclipses reflection, quiet replacement may proceed unnoticed.

The future is not predetermined. Coexistence requires vigilance, adaptability, and a commitment to preserving uniquely human contributions. Replacement becomes likely only when humans relinquish responsibility. In an AI-driven world, sustaining relevance is less about resisting technology and more about defining its role thoughtfully.

Preserving Human Agency in an AI World

As Artificial Intelligence becomes embedded in daily life, the most pressing question is not what machines can do, but what humans will continue to decide. Agency—the capacity to act intentionally, to choose freely, and to bear responsibility for those choices—is central to human dignity. In an AI-mediated world, preserving agency requires more than technological awareness; it demands deliberate cultural, educational, and institutional effort.

AI systems increasingly recommend, predict, automate, and optimize. They suggest routes, curate information, generate content, and assess risk. These systems are designed for efficiency and personalization. Yet efficiency can gradually replace reflection. When decisions become easier through automation, individuals may engage less actively in the process. The convenience of delegation can erode intentionality.

Preserving agency begins with awareness. Individuals must recognize that algorithmic outputs are not neutral truths but products of design choices and data patterns. Understanding that recommendations are shaped by objectives—engagement, profitability, safety—introduces critical distance. Without this awareness, obedience becomes habitual.

Education plays a foundational role. In an AI-driven world, literacy extends beyond reading and writing to include algorithmic literacy. Students must learn how intelligent systems function, how biases can be encoded, and how to evaluate outputs critically. Teaching individuals to question and contextualize AI responses reinforces cognitive independence.

Agency also depends on friction. Friction—pausing before accepting a recommendation, exploring alternatives, questioning assumptions—creates space for deliberate choice. While AI minimizes friction to streamline interaction, humans must reintroduce it consciously. Choosing to reflect rather than react preserves autonomy.

Institutional design influences agency as well. Organizations must ensure that AI systems augment rather than override human judgment. Decision-making frameworks should allow for human oversight and override mechanisms. Transparency in how systems operate fosters accountability. When individuals can understand and challenge outputs, agency strengthens.

Another dimension involves redefining value. If society equates worth solely with efficiency, humans may feel compelled to align with algorithmic standards. Preserving agency requires valuing qualities that machines cannot replicate fully—empathy, ethical reasoning, creativity rooted in experience. Recognizing these attributes as central to human contribution reinforces identity beyond performance metrics.

Emotional resilience is equally important. As AI systems outperform humans in certain tasks, comparison may undermine confidence. Preserving agency involves reframing collaboration as empowerment rather than competition. Machines extend capability; they do not define purpose.

Public policy also shapes agency. Regulatory frameworks that mandate transparency, protect privacy, and enforce accountability ensure that AI systems serve human interests. Without governance, control may concentrate in institutions that design and deploy intelligence. Democratic oversight preserves collective agency.

Cultural narratives influence perception. If technology is portrayed as inevitable and autonomous, individuals may feel powerless. If framed as a tool shaped by human intention, agency remains central. Storytelling, media, and education must emphasize human responsibility in guiding AI development.

Preserving agency does not mean rejecting AI. It means engaging with it consciously. Collaboration can enhance productivity and insight, but delegation must be intentional. Humans must remain authors of goals, interpreters of results, and guardians of ethics.

The challenge is subtle because erosion of agency is gradual. Each automated decision, each unquestioned recommendation, slightly shifts responsibility outward. Over time, habits form. Recognizing these shifts early prevents deeper dependency.

Agency also involves moral courage. When algorithmic outputs conflict with ethical judgment, individuals must be willing to question and override. Systems should not become shields that absolve responsibility.

Ultimately, preserving human agency in an AI world requires balance. Technology can enhance life, but autonomy must remain non-negotiable. Intentionality, reflection, and accountability distinguish human thought from computational process.

The future of AI integration will reflect collective choices. If humans remain vigilant, informed, and ethically engaged, agency will endure. If convenience eclipses consciousness, autonomy may diminish.

In the end, Artificial Intelligence is powerful—but it is not sovereign. Human beings design it, deploy it, and live with its consequences. Preserving agency means remembering that responsibility cannot be automated. Choice remains human.

www.ingramcontent.com/pod-product-compliance
Lightning Source LLC
Chambersburg PA
CBHW041300210926
51847CB00009B/88
9789699797484